DEDICATION

With love to Jennine, Maggie, and DB

Core 5® Marketing

Proven Strategies For Growing Your Business

Gordon Van Wechel

Copyright © 2020 Gordon Van Wechel

All rights reserved.

ISBN: 9798623505224

Core 5® is a registered trademark of
The Alchemy Consulting Group

CONTENTS

	Acknowledgments	i
1	Introduction	1
2	Foundations	5
3	Your Profit Funnel	33
4	Reputation Marketing	47
5	Paid Traffic	65
6	Social Media	89
7	Video Marketing	99
8	Getting Found Online	119
9	What Now?	131
10	11 Questions	135

ACKNOWLEDGMENTS

Over the years I've had the benefit of working with many creative entrepreneurs and business owners.   Thanks to each of them for the lessons that have helped my career, which I'm now passing on.

Introduction

When I was in graduate school one of my professors was fond of saying that whenever we read a book or listen to a speaker or read an article in an industry magazine one of the things we should always do is determine the authors bias. What is their frame of reference? Why do they reach conclusions they want you to accept? How did they choose the data they offer as proof of their position? Are they hoping to sell you something? Or convert you to a particular belief?

As you read this book, I'm going to save you struggling with that issue and tell you right up front what I believe about marketing and the challenge of being a business owner in today's difficult economic climate. I wish I could claim it as original, but it is a statement I heard from the late Peter Drucker. He said, **"there are only two important activities for a business owner to be involved in: marketing and innovation. Everything else can be delegated."**

Marketing is sharing what your company does and inspiring people to do business with you. Innovation is making sure that your company is responsive to the changing wants of your customers and is the best that it can be. According to Professor Drucker these are the only activities that we as business owners should be focused on.

I understand how easy it seems for a university professor to make a statement like that. He's never worked 80-hour weeks, struggled to make payroll, and missed family activities to solve a customer service issue. Those of us who have been entrepreneurs know all too well about those times, particularly in the early days of starting our company.

Yet, I believe that ultimately Professor Drucker was right. As your business comes out of that initial "survival mode," as you identify some key people to help you and achieve a degree of stability, your focus as the owner must change if you are to create a sustainable enterprise. Most of us who have started a business have the vision that we are creating an asset that sometime in the future we can sell or turn over to a good manager and enjoy the fruits of our labor.

To make that happen we must transition from working so hard "in" our business and begin to work "on" our business. That means we need to step back from making all the decisions and focus on innovating our company to be the best it can be, and then implement the most effective marketing strategies so customers can find us.

I've written this book to help you identify some of the best marketing strategies for a business or professional practice. These have been proven in "real world" situations with hundreds of our clients in many business niches and geographical markets across the country since I started Alchemy in 2003.

I will be suggesting a diversity of marketing channels you might consider. If you are a newer business, or still small, do not be intimidated by this! Clients that have been with us for more than five years started quite small with one or two initial strategies. As they grew, we grew with them, adding services and channels as they had the capacity to handle growth and the budget to drive it. One of our Core Values as a company is, "We Want to be Your In-House Marketing Department."

As you will read, most of the focus of the book is on digital marketing strategies. The Internet has become the "go to" place for a business to find new customers. That is not to say that there are no other valuable channels that can be used to accomplish your objectives. But particularly for businesses doing less than $3 million in annual revenue, the Internet offers the best option for business growth at a consistent rate with a reasonable budget spend.

This is not a book about marketing theory. I'm going to share with you exactly what we do when implementing Core 5® for our clients. I encourage you, as you are reading, to take notes and consider how to put these strategies into practice. In the back of the book is some information about our company and a way to contact me directly. In fact, I'm offering readers a free one-hour opportunity to talk with me about your business. I encourage you to do so.

To Your Success!

Gordon

A note on terms I use. I recognize that some business niches refer to themselves as a business, others as a Professional Practice or Medical Practice. For the sake of simplicity I will use "business" most of the time, but understand that I am describing all three types of business entity.

In the same way I will use "customer" most of the time, even though I am aware that you may refer to your patrons as "clients" or "patients."

"You will attract way more buyers if you are offering to teach them something of value to them than you ever will attract by simply trying to sell them your product or service."

--Chet Holmes

Foundations: Know Your Business

When you think about growing your business or professional practice, what comes to mind? Where is the best place to buy advertising? Should I open an office in another city? If I decide to add a new product line will that dilute my brand? I know I need to be online these days, but how do I do that?

All good questions. But they are the wrong questions!

Let me share an experience I had a few years ago after speaking at a marketing seminar in Denver. After my presentation I stayed around to talk with attendees and maybe find a client or two. As I was chatting with several people, a man came up to the group and was obviously anxious to talk. As people drifted away, he pulled me aside and blurted out, "I've signed a contract for a full-page ad in the Yellow Pages for the next year and my ad is due tomorrow. How much will you charge me to write the ad?"

Without a pause I said, "$2,000."

"What!" he gasped. "Two grand just to write an ad for the Yellow Pages? That's crazy!"

"Really?" I said. "Think about it. I don't know you. I don't know your company and the products you offer. I don't know your customer, your value proposition, or other advertising you do. If all you want is a list of platitudes and generalities to give the Yellow Pages rep, you certainly don't need me. But if you want the $40,000 you're going to spend over the next year on that full-page ad to actually give you a return on that investment, then I have to know all of those details about your business so I can write an ad that will attract the prospects you want."

I didn't get the job that day. But – interestingly enough, that same business owner called me several months later, asked for a meeting, and did hire our company to help them introduce a new product line.

That experience is not unusual. In fact, far too often when I begin a conversation with a prospective client about marketing their business, they immediately want to talk tactics. "Do you think cable television is a good place to advertise? The local company is offering some great programs." My response to these questions is always the same: "It could be. We'll have to do the research before we can know for sure."

I'm going to say the same thing to you as you begin reading this book on marketing your business. You probably picked it up because you want to grow your business but aren't really certain how to get started. In fact, I'll bet this isn't the first "marketing" book you've opened. The reality is that all kinds of "gurus" are offering you the latest and greatest strategy you can read. It's true that any number of marketing tactics could work for you, but they might not be the best for your company at this time with the marketing budget you have available.

In this opening chapter, I'm going to share with you the foundation of our marketing philosophy here at The Alchemy Consulting Group. I think this is a necessary first step because I want you to feel confident that the information you're about to receive is credible and accurate and, most importantly, will make you money.

The bookstore shelves are full of books from people who are great at writing books but short on experience when it comes to real-world results. I challenge you to go to your favorite bookstore and find more than one or two books that actually have useful advertising advice and examples that are of any relevance to you in your situation when trying to implement them into your business. I know, because I've spent hours at Barnes and Noble poring over book after book in the sales, advertising, and marketing sections. I've scanned and read through hundreds of websites of so-called advertising experts. Through all that, I've found only a handful of what I would call authoritative guides to getting results – that is, making real-world money – through marketing.

So, I'll make you a few promises right now, right up front. First, I promise you that everything you will learn in this book will be applicable to you as the owner or executive in a real-world business or professional practice, no matter what size you are now. I promise you that you won't find yourself wondering, "What in the heck does that have to do with my business?" I promise you that all the examples I share come from real-life, hands-on experience. I promise you if you will implement the strategies that I'm going to share, you will see an immediate impact in the effectiveness of your marketing.

Or, in other words, I promise you that this stuff will make you money. And that's the name of the game, right? I don't suppose you picked up a program on marketing for any other reason than to learn how to make more money, did you?

The title of this chapter is "Know Your Business," and in the next few pages I'm going to share with you eight marketing concepts that form the bedrock of the Alchemy philosophy. They are

- What Marketing is Supposed to Do
- The Inside Reality of Your Company vs. the Outside Perception of the Marketplace
- Defined versus Non-Defined Market
- Identifying your Ideal Customer/Client/Patient
- Strategic Marketing and Tactical Marketing
- The Educational Spectrum
- Articulating Your Value Proposition
- Key Metrics for Running Your Business

I want to begin with these rather than jump ahead and show you how to design a lead generation website or build an effective pay-per-click campaign. We'll get to some tremendously powerful strategies for growing your company, but not until you understand *why* they can have such an impact.

What Marketing is Supposed to Do

I have started many of my presentations to industry groups or business audiences with this simple question: What is marketing supposed to do?

I'll typically let several people offer their answers, and they'll range from "get a new customer" to "introduce a product" to "grow my brand" to "enhance my reputation" and more.

You know what? All of these are correct; I wouldn't argue with any of them. But these answers really describe the *results* of a properly designed marketing campaign. So, what's the right answer? What is it that marketing is really supposed to accomplish for my business?

Simply put, three things:

1. Capture the attention of your target market
2. Facilitate the prospects information gathering and decision-making process
3. Lower the risk of taking the next step in the sales cycle

I'll be talking more about each of these throughout this book. For now though, the point I want you to consider and remember is that as a business owner, your job is to step back from the day-to-day management of the business and think about what is in the mind of your prospects, and then design your marketing to help them answer their questions.

Inside Reality vs. Outside Perception

Your business really has two different sides. First, there's what I call the "*Inside Reality*," and second, there is the "*Outside Perception*." The Inside Reality has to do with all the things your business does that makes you valuable to your customers, from the materials you use and your business operations to the commitment to excellence of your management team. It's what gives you a competitive advantage in the marketplace.

We call it the *Inside Reality* because there's a good chance that the reality of what you do and the customers' perceptions of what you do aren't necessarily the same. You'll find that these two words – reality and perception – are very important to this process of winning the market share war for your business.

The Inside Reality encompasses everything you do and everything you are that makes you good. It's all your skills, your people, your expertise, your service to the customer (before, during, *and* after the sale), your systems, your operational procedures, your commitment to exceed customer expectations, your passion, and the way you conduct your business.

Now, you might think you're better than you are, or you might not be giving yourself enough credit for the things you do well. But there is a reality of how valuable you are to the marketplace based on these things and others, both tangible and intangible. That is what we call the "Inside Reality."

If you asked your customers why they bought from you, they could tell you something quantifiable, specific, and instantly obvious. They could point to specific advantages of doing business with you and say, "That's why I use you, that's why I refer my friends to you, that's why I'm a fan of your company." It's imperative that you begin to innovate your company so that there's a reason for people to choose you. But here's the problem: Just because you've achieved that level of innovation doesn't mean that customers are going to flock to your business. There's still a job of marketing that must be done. And that's where the "Outside Perception" comes into play.

If the Inside Reality is about what you do and what you are that allows your business to perform better, then the *Outside Perception* has to do with how customers and prospects perceive your industry and then your company. Invariably, the Inside Reality and the Outside Perception are different. And the truth is, regardless of how good you are, most of your prospects are not going to give a thought to – much less care about – your Inside Reality. Not because they don't like you or they think your business is bad; it's because trying to figure what makes you good (assuming you're good!) is the last thing on their priority list.

Ask yourself this question: how many competitors, either direct or indirect, do you have in your business? Whatever that number is, that's how many choices your prospects have, and how many businesses they must sift through to try to make a buying decision.

Add in the general perception about your industry, which in many cases trends toward the negative, and the marketing battle for a company with an excellent Inside Reality is even more difficult. The problem is that most businesses don't have the ability to communicate via advertising and marketing their Inside Reality to the outside world. You can't lead prospects to the conclusion that they would have to be an absolute fool to do business with anyone else but you … even if you *are* that good.

That is the challenge of marketing your business, conveying the excellent Inside Reality of your company to a marketplace that tends to look at all businesses in your niche as basically the same.

The late business speaker Jim Rohn might have summed it up best in his lecture about communications. He was talking about personal communication, not business, but I think the principles are identical. He said that to be a master communicator, all you've got to do is follow this simple three-step process: First, have something good to say. Second, say it well. And third, say it often. Does that make sense to you? Have something good to say, say it well, and say it often.

Having something good to say is the Inside Reality of your business, the excellent people and systems that you have created. My purpose in writing this book is to improve the Outside Perception of your business – in other words, how to say it well, so people will choose your company for the product or service they are searching for.

Sometimes when I share these concepts, a business owner will say, "Yes, okay, that makes sense to me. The Inside Reality and the Outside Perception. But will these marketing strategies work for ME in MY business?" The answer is an unqualified "YES!" Over the years we have worked with hundreds of companies in a variety of industries, and what I see is that on the most basic level all business owners want the same thing: more new customers and less competition. They want to keep their margins, have their marketing and advertising work better, attract and retain more loyal customers, increase the conversion ratios for their salespeople, and ultimately, they all want to make more money. True enough?

Now. I want you to also recognize that all of your prospects and customers want the same things. They want to get the best deal, in terms of price and value. They want to feel confident that their money has been well spent and their decision has been made to the best of their ability. You never hear anybody say, "I got bids from five car dealers and negotiated the best prices I could, and finally decided to buy where I got the third-best deal." No! People instinctively want to make the best decision possible.

So we have two sets of values: the business wants more customers and loyal customers, and the customer wants the best possible deal, in terms of overall value. The process and principles that govern the matching of those two sets of values are the same for every business. It's simple: all you have to do as the business owner is give prospects a reason to believe that you are actually the best deal, in terms of price and value, and then communicate those reasons to them in a way that they will pay attention to and believe.

The problem is that most companies come nowhere close to holding up their end of the bargain. Most have a tough time distinguishing and differentiating their business, and then communicating those advantages in an instantly obvious way. They can't make their Outside Perception match their Inside Reality.

Think of it this way. What if you could find a way to generate 20% more qualified leads for your business than you do right now, without increasing your monthly ad spend? Assuming you kept your same closing ratio, what would 20% more qualified leads for the same money spent mean to your bottom line? And then consider this: what if you could draw in 20% more qualified prospects, but you could ALSO find a way to increase your conversion ratio by 10% – across the board? What would THAT do to your bottom line? I'm going to go way out on a limb and say that you might be able to achieve those kinds of modest increases just by reading this book and implementing some of the marketing strategies I'm going to teach you.

Defined vs. Non-Defined Market

Knowing where to find your customers is critical to managing your ad budget. Essential to this is defining your market. Let me first explain the difference between a defined and a non-defined market. Then I'll give you a technique for identifying who your ideal customer really is.

A defined marketplace is one for which you can identify, pinpoint, and obtain a list of people that are prospects for your business. A non-defined market is just the opposite: you have to go out and advertise to create leads to begin the marketing process.

Let me elaborate. If you sell business to business, like we do here at Alchemy Consulting, then it is pretty easy to define a market. For example, if I want to market our company's services to plumbers in Omaha, I can go to any number of sources and buy a list of all the plumbing contractors in that city. I can specify the annual sales volume of the company, or the number of employees they have, how long they've been in business, and so on. Then I can design a marketing campaign that is focused on the needs typically faced by plumbing contractors in growing their businesses. Easy, right?

Some things aren't that simple, though. What if you are a chiropractor in Denver? Do you have any way to know who woke up that morning with back pain and thought, "I should find a chiropractor and get some relief for this aching back"?

Not likely.

Or what if you're a Lasik eye surgeon in Sacramento. How can you possibly know the people in your market area who are tired of wearing glasses or contacts and wonder if Lasik will help? You can't.

The challenge of a non-defined market is that you must spend much of your advertising budget collecting leads. That significantly changes your strategies.

Which leads us to the next topic.

Identifying Your Ideal Customer

This might seem obvious, and you might be saying to yourself, "My ideal customer is someone who needs what I sell." I agree, but by just generalizing your customer to be anyone who needs your product or service, you force yourself into spending your marketing budget advertising for leads. I spoke about this in the previous section when I introduced the concept of defined or non-defined marketing for your product or service.

The more precisely you can define your marketplace, the more effective your marketing will be, and the more profitable your business is going to be. I don't know if he originated the statement, but the late Dan Kennedy was the person I heard say, "If everybody is your customer, then nobody is your customer." If you stop and think about that for a minute, it makes sense. If you are trying to sell landscaping services to anyone and everyone in your city, you have a tough challenge unless you have a huge marketing budget. Narrowing that market down and identifying specific people or groups who are potential targets makes your marketing much more effective. How do you do that? Here are several ideas:

1. If you're in a service business, what services do you offer? Make a list. For example, if you're an attorney who specializes in trusts, what else do you have expertise in? What about helping a business with a succession plan? Or working with the business owner to negotiate the sale of the business?

    Or suppose you're a roofing contractor. Do you only do roof replacement, or do you also offer repair services? Is roofing your only business, or do you have another related product or service (such as siding and windows, concrete flatwork, or gutter install)? Do you have a completely different business during the winter? Start the ideal customer identification process by first segmenting the different businesses you have. Each one has one or more ideal customers you can specifically identify and market to.

2. Think about the demographics in your market area. What part(s) of town are you currently getting most of your business from? Is that where you really want to be? Are their neighborhoods or surrounding communities that you would like to have more jobs in? Are you typically getting $5,000 jobs when there are neighborhoods in your city that would have $8,000 or $12,000 jobs?

3. As you begin to think about your ideal customer, ask yourself where they gather in the greatest numbers. What other companies or organizations transact

business with them? How can you obtain or build a list using their other involvements?

4. How do they like to be communicated with? What do they read? Listen to?

The easiest way to begin to identify your ideal customer is to look at the customers you have done business with during the past year. Here are some questions to ask about them:

- Who made the decision? What is their gender, age, income, occupation?
- Where, exactly, did they live? (Get a map of your area and use pushpins to locate every customer's address.)
- How did they hear about you? How did they contact you? Or did you make the initial contact with them?
- Why did they buy from you rather than a competitor? Be honest with yourself here. If you are willing to discount your price to get the job, then recognize that fact.
- What, if any, continuing contact have you had with the customer since finishing their job?

Now, what do you do with this data? First, you should be able to quantify some information about your company and the success of your marketing efforts as a result of doing this analysis.

As you look at the customer profile that emerges, ask yourself if that is who you want to continue to market to. If so, then you're going to be pleased with the strategies I'll be sharing with you in the coming chapters. They will help you target your ideal customers more accurately and at a lower cost than much of what you are doing today.

If not — if you want to grow your business with a different level of customer — then I'm going to show you how to do that as well. Here's a quick example. We worked with an HVAC contractor who had a good-sized business in many of the middle-class neighborhoods on the west side of his city. He asked if we could help him break into some of the suburbs on the south side, where most of the executive homes were located. After analyzing the market, we designed campaigns using online banner ads focused on the geographical area he wanted to generate business in. We were able to place his ads in front of homeowners in those neighborhoods as they went online. The cost was very reasonable, roughly $35 for a thousand impressions! Within a few weeks he began to get calls from the south side. The profit from his first job paid his entire marketing budget for the year!

Do you offer a type or level of service that's different from many of your competitors? Here's an example of what I mean by this question. We helped a roofing contractor identify a niche of small apartment properties, twelve units or less, throughout his city. We obtained a list of the building owners and also identified several property-management companies who worked with these owners. We created a series of marketing pieces highlighting his company's expertise with this level of building and began reaching out to both owners and management firms, offering a free roof inspection. In this case about 20% of the owners did not live in the area and were grateful to have a licensed professional monitoring the condition of the roofs of their investments.

His follow-up offer was for an annual maintenance contract "to extend the life of their roof." We set up a program of contacting these building owners four times each year with this offer. Over time he had more than twenty buildings "under contract" at between $400 and $900 a year for inspections every six months. His total cost for the marketing plan was less than $2500 for the year! Oh, and every time one of these roofs needed to be replaced, guess who got the business without having to bid against other contractors? That's right, our client.

Were the inspections every six months a problem? No. When a crew finished a job early, or had the occasional slow week, he'd send them to inspect using the checklist we'd developed. They would take photos using their cell phones. He would then use their information and pictures to prepare a short report for the building owner and manager. In fact, his office manager did the reports and sent them out for him! All he did was read and sign.

What I'm suggesting you do is consider how many "market niches" you can identify in your local area. The more you can focus your marketing on these smaller groups, the higher your return on monthly ad spend.

Strategic Marketing and Tactical Marketing

As the owner of your business or professional practice, you must understand the distinction between strategic and tactical marketing. This is important because you want to focus your time where it is most effective. Most business owners concentrate on tactical marketing; I want to encourage you to give your attention to strategic marketing. Let me begin by defining what those terms mean.

Strategic marketing is what you say, how you say it, and who you say it to. Tactical marketing is where you say it. Let me put it another way. Strategic marketing is your marketing plan. It is how you define and identify your ideal customer, the target market(s) that you are selling to, and the things that you are going to say that are specifically relevant to those people. Tactical marketing is how you are going to find them. That might mean radio advertising, or changing your website, or doing demographic display ads on the internet; that's the tactical side.

I know from experience with a lot of business owners that you spend most of your time on the tactical. Here's an example. You decide to run a seasonal promotion, which means you will need to put a display ad into the local newspaper. Immediately you put together some ideas for the ad, then call the salesperson at the newspaper to help you with layout. They are more than happy to take your money and put your ad in for the weekend. By the middle of the next week you are scratching your head and wondering why the phone hasn't been ringing.

Has that ever been your experience?

Here's why. We spend our time on tactical marketing (where to say it), when what we really ought to be doing is stepping back and focusing on the strategic side (what you say, how you say it, and who you say it to.) One of the people from whom I learned marketing years ago had a phrase I want to share that with you. What he used to say was, "If you want to know what John Smith buys, you have to see the world through John Smith's eyes." Here is what he meant. As a business owner, you must understand what is important to your customers, the "conversation going on in their minds," so that you can address their desires.

Instead, here is what most of us do. We know our product and service really well, we know our company and how good we are, so that's the frame of reference we use in our marketing. We write ads that makes sense to *us*, that have a lot of "features," without paying attention to the "benefits" our customer is actually looking for. This is why you see so many ads with ludicrous platitudes saying things like, "we are the best," "in business for 39 years," "we do quality work," and "our staff is friendly." Are statements like these of any value to a prospect who is deciding whether to do business with your company or a competitor? NO!

As a business owner, how do you know how John Smith sees the world? How do you know what John Smith's eyes are looking for? Simple: you ask John. When we work with a client, we get a list of recent customers and, with the customers' permission, interview them, asking a series of fourteen questions designed to help us uncover their real motivations. Let me offer three of the most important and encourage you to have some conversations with your recent customers.

1. Under what circumstances does the typical prospect begin to think about buying your product or service?

Sometimes this is obvious, like when their pet is sick and they need a veterinarian. But what about the person who is thinking about selling their home in a year and wants to see if the furnace is efficient enough to get through the sales and inspection process? Or the business owner who is wondering how to organize his business so his two sons can take over when he is ready to retire in five years? Each one of these prospects has a different motivation, and it will take a unique marketing message to reach them.

2. What things are important to your prospects when purchasing what you sell?

Again, the simple answer might be price or materials or convenience. But you also need to think about the buying process. What is important to your prospects when they go through the process of buying what you offer? What are steps in the process that might be challenging for your customers? If they don't buy your product or service very often, just knowing the right questions to ask is a challenge.

Think about what your customers want, *as well as what they want to avoid*. In your marketing you want to address all those issues, both factual and experiential. (Here's a personal example. I hate the process of buying a car. The thought of going onto a car lot, dealing with a salesperson, listening to their drivel about the features of the vehicle that mean nothing to me, completing the paperwork – yuck! I'm the perfect candidate for one of the businesses that goes out and finds a car for me and negotiates everything. They charge $500 or more for their service, and I'll gladly pay it to avoid the shopping experience myself.)

3. What are the relevant and important issues that a prospect needs to be aware of when making a decision about what you sell?

What are the challenges that John and Jane Smith are having as they come into your world, and what can you do to innovate your company to address those challenges in a way that is comfortable for the Smiths?

All three of these questions are strategic – that is, they focus on John Smith's desires, his "hot buttons." I recognize that hot button is kind of an old-school term. Today you might think of it as what are the keywords prospective customers would use when they search on Google? Don't assume that you know the answer to that question. Even for a task as simple as finding a plumber or dentist, people will use a variety of search terms.

Now, let's look at another question: Where did your customers look for a company in your niche? That is, how did you find us and call for information?

This question, unlike the three above, is tactical. Again, the easy answer is "Google" or any of the search engines. But while it is true that many internet searches are done each day in your niche, that is not the only answer. Once you know where most of your customers are looking, and the search terms they are using, you'll know where to invest your marketing budget for the highest return.

The Educational Spectrum

To help me explain this concept I want to share a story about my father. When he retired, my parents moved to Arizona and bought a home in a nice neighborhood near Phoenix. Like many of the communities in that area, the landscaping was primarily rock yards with varieties of cactus and fruit trees, but no grass.

I was sitting in my Denver office one day in late March. It was snowing and I'd had a difficult time even getting to the office that morning. About 9 am my dad called to say hello. During the course of our conversation he shared that he had just stepped out into his back yard and pulled a fresh grapefruit off the tree and was about to enjoy it for breakfast. Here I am sitting in the snow and cold and he's enjoying a fresh grapefruit! I grumbled some response, said good-bye, and went back to work.

Let me ask you a question. When Dad went out and picked his grapefruit that morning, were all of the fruits on the tree equally ripe and ready to eat? Or course not. More than likely there were quite a few ready, others that were still a little green and needed more time, and still more that had already ripened to the point where they fell off the tree and were lying on the ground.

Isn't it the same with prospects for your business? Some are just starting their thought process about buying what you sell. Others are in the market asking questions and gathering information so they can make a good decision. Still others know what they want and have their credit card in hand. They just need to find a vendor.

Why then do you market to every prospect with exactly the same message? Wouldn't it make more sense to offer valuable information that answers the questions of prospects who are just starting to search for your service? Then keep dripping informative content and "building a relationship" with them as they continue their search? And then make compelling offers to them as they get close to making a decision?

We call this a "marketing funnel," and I have a complete discussion on how to build this type of marketing architecture later in this book. For now, I want you to recognize that your prospects are individuals who have their own questions and timelines for making a decision. If you are going to win the competitive battle of earning their business, then you need to stop trying to put everyone into the same box and start thinking of them as individuals who are somewhere along the Educational Spectrum getting ready to make a buying decision.

Articulating Your Value Proposition

The final piece to your well-constructed marketing foundation is to define your value proposition. That is, "Why should a prospect choose your company instead of your competitors?" One of the reasons I suggested you spend time identifying your ideal customer(s) is because it is very likely that you will have a different value proposition for each customer. The value proposition should answer the question "Why should I buy *this* product or service?" as well as "Why should I do anything at all?" It is a clear and specific statement about the tangible benefits of your offer and should be stated in terms understood and accepted by the target customer.

To begin, I'll suggest a way to think through and write out your value proposition. Then I'll give you some examples for different customers. The first portion of the value proposition asserts the value of the offering in terms of the results and benefits, and it demonstrates how you are equipped to deliver that value (it notes your skills and abilities). The second sentence asserts the positioning of that value by establishing a contrast.

First Sentence:

- Because we have *(skills, experience, knowledge, or other attribute)*
- We are able to *(provide service, fix the problem, or other deliverable).*
- This means *(benefits the client will value)*
- For *(the client)*

Second (optional) Sentence:

- Unlike *(primary competitive alternative),*
- Our service *(statement of primary differentiation).*

Here are some examples taken from a roofing company in a large market in Minnesota.

First, for a homeowner in a mid-range neighborhood:

"Because we have superior materials buying power made possible by the number of jobs we do each year, we are able to offer you top-quality 30-year roofing shingles at the same price as the lower quality 20-year. This means that you will have a better, longer-lasting roof, and we'll be able to complete the job using the funds allocated by your insurance company without you paying anything out of your pocket other than your deductible."

Second, for a property investor:

"Because we have superior materials buying power made possible by the number of jobs we do each year, we can replace the roof less expensively and get materials delivered to the site within 48 hours. This means the job will be done quickly and at a lower cost, enabling you to flip the property at a higher margin."

Third, for homeowner in a higher-end neighborhood:

"As a market leader here in (your town), we enjoy superior buying power made possible by the number of jobs we do each year. This enables us to offer you the best possible materials for your job, in a variety of finishes and colors to enhance the street appeal of your home. Our crews have experience in the finish details around skylights, chimneys, and vents so you can rely on the quality of the workmanship. This means you will have a better, longer-lasting roof, with the job completed on time."

I hope you are beginning to see the importance of a clear value proposition tailored to each type of customer you work with. A value proposition cannot be a series of platitudes and generalities. It must draw a line in the sand between you and your competitors, as well as clearly state the benefit to the customer of working with your company.

No matter what type of business you own, being able to articulate a clear value proposition for each of the products or services you offer is critical to attracting the ideal customer you want to serve. Use the simple outline I've suggested as a starting point. At the end of the book there is an offer for a free, one-hour marketing consultation. I'd be happy to help you identify your ideal customers and refine your value propositions.

Key Metrics for Running Your Business

I'm sorry, but now we have to talk about math. This was my

worst subject in school, and I still struggle with it, but I would be doing you a disservice if I didn't point out some critical statistics that you need to know about your business to be able to market it effectively.

The first is the *average transaction value* that your customers spend with you. This is a simple calculation: take your total sales and divide by the number of sales. If you did $10,000 in sales and had 100 customers, then your average transaction value is $100.

Of course, it's not really that simple. Most businesses have a variety of products and services at different price points. How do you calculate an average transaction value in this case?

If that describes your business, then you want to organize your products or services into "like price" groups. For example, you sell a variety of products between $75 and $200. Another set of your products are in the $400 to $600 range, and you have a few higher-end products at around $1,000. You would identify three averages: $125, $500, and $1,000.

Three different average transaction values mean you're going analyze your marketing based on each product group. How much are you willing to invest to attract a customer to each?

The second metric is *lifetime value of a customer*. Most businesses and professional practices work with a customer or client more than once over a period of years. If a customer buys four times a year, stays with you for three years, and typically purchases products in the middle range ($500 in our example), then the lifetime value of that customer is $500 x 4 purchases a year x 3 years = $6,000.

Knowing these two key performance indicators for your business is critical to helping you decide how much you can spend on marketing. Let me elaborate on that, continuing with the example from the last paragraph. If you have a customer who spends $6,000 with you over a three-year period, how much are you willing to spend to attract that customer? Most business owners only look at the initial transaction, the $500. They calculate their profit margin on that transaction at 30%, or $150, and answer the question with a percentage of the $150 profit margin.

That would be a short-sighted calculation! The reality is that this customer, on average, is worth $1,800 to your business ($6,000 x 30%). Now answer the question again. How much are you willing to spend to acquire a customer who is worth $1,800 to you? The answer is very likely going to be more than the $150 profit you make on the first sale.

Why am I making such a point of this? Simple. There is an absolute rule in business that says, "The company that can spend the most to acquire a new customer will win the battle every time." Think about it. If you know these two metrics for your business and are willing to outspend your competitors to earn the new customers coming into the marketplace, your competitors will slowly starve.

I can hear the objection in your mind. It goes something like this: "But Gordon, not every customer that comes in will stay with me for three years. Some might never come back, and I'd lose money on them." That is true, and that is why I talk about the average transaction value and average lifetime value of a customer.

But here's the secret to making these numbers work in your favor: make the Inside Reality of your company so compelling that once customers experience your service, they won't think of going to the competition, regardless of pricing offered.

There is another objection that I often hear from owners in the building trades. "I remodel kitchens. Once I do a kitchen, that customer doesn't need me again. I don't have a lifetime value; I'm a 'one and done' business." Here again I agree, with this caveat. If you never talk with that customer again, you are one and done. But what if you put a comprehensive and well-thought-out referral program in place? A process by which you followed up periodically with your past customers, giving them valuable tips on keeping their new kitchen looking new as well as asking for a referral to their friends and neighbors who might be thinking of a new kitchen?

Let me tell you two quick stories. We worked with a roofing contractor in the Seattle area. His average job was $16,000. We designed a multi-step, two-year follow-up campaign resulting in referrals that we tracked back to the initial customer. At the end of the two years, his transaction value had increase to just under $20,000, almost a 25% increase in an industry that is perceived as "one and done."

Second example: a remodeling contractor who did a lot of kitchens. At the conclusion of each job, she asked the homeowner to invite 20 to 30 of their close friends over for a party to show off their new kitchen. The contractor hired a caterer who provided food, beverages, and staff, making it zero work or expense for the client. At the party, the contractor made it a point to interact with each couple attending, pointing out some of the design and workmanship details of the new kitchen. She never had less than three appointments with new prospects after each party. These contacts resulted in at least one job, at an average job size of $35,000!

I don't believe in "one and done." There is always a way to implement a marketing strategy that will increase the potential value of a customer.

I've spent a lot of time in this chapter sharing some foundational concepts for marketing your business or professional practice. I hope you've read them carefully, because as we begin to discuss more of the specific marketing channels and strategies that might make sense to implement in your enterprise, I want you to be able to evaluate them using the definitions established.

Now, let's jump into the Core 5®!

Core 5® Marketing

"What do you want from me? Fine writing? Or do you want to see the sales curve stop moving down and start moving up?

--Rosser Reeves

Your Profit Funnel—Websites on Steroids

If you were to take a one question survey of small business owners, asking the question: "what is your primary marketing tool?" what do you think the answer would be? Most would answer something about their website. That seems logical in this digital age where so many search for products and services online. Would it surprise you to know that 36% of all small businesses in the US still <u>do not</u> have a website? What is more interesting is that number has stayed consistent over the last five years.

The fact that you're reading this book tells me you're in the 64% that do have at least a basic "brochure" style website for your business. But I could be wrong about that. Regardless of which side of that spectrum your business is on, in this chapter I want to introduce you to the concept of a "profit funnel." If you don't have a website, then this information will help you design a productive sequence of online marketing tools that can generate new prospects every day. If you currently have a website then I'm going to show you ways to make it even more productive.

First things first: what is a Profit Funnel? It is simply a process that is designed to move a prospect through the sales process.

"Doesn't my website do that already?" you ask. Only partially. Your website most likely lists all the products or services you offer, has information about your company, maybe a video or two, a page for interested prospects to contact you, and perhaps a blog. The developer who created the site for you probably used Word Press, Joomla, or another of the more common website building platforms. No matter how it was built, most likely there is a menu bar across the top of the Home page that the visitor can click on to be taken to another page on your site. This traditional "horizontal" architecture is how websites have been built from the beginning of the Internet.

The question that you must ask as a business owner is this. "Does my website take a prospect through the sales process, answering their questions, helping them reach the decision to do business with my company?" For most businesses that are not just offering a 'commodity' or low-priced product the answer is no. If you have a medical or dental practice, are an attorney, contractor, any business that offers a product that most buyers research before making a buying decision; then your website is not a profit funnel.

When your prospect is doing their research what questions are in their minds? What information are they seeking? What are their dreams/goals/hopes they want to fulfill with the product or service they are searching for? How does your website meet the needs of each of these prospects? In most cases, it doesn't. That's why a profit funnel is imperative if you want to increase market share and profitability.

I want to take a minute and share more about this "buyers journey" concept. When someone goes online and begins to look at websites they have five questions in mind that need to be answered before they contact a supplier. These are:

- Will this solve my problem?
- Do I have to decide now?
- Am I getting the best?
- Am I going to regret this?
- Am I paying a good price?

Here are additional interesting facts about the web searches your prospects are making:

> 62% of all traffic now comes from a mobile device. (Source: Right Edge)
>
> 88% of consumers that search using a mobile device call or visit that business within 24 hours. (Source: Nectafy)
>
> 77% of customers will stop engaging with content that doesn't display well on their device. (Source: Ironpaper)
>
> New research by Google has found that 53% of mobile website users will leave a webpage if it doesn't load within 3 seconds (Source: DoubleClick)
>
> Users on a mobile device scroll with just their thumb. Clicking is not convenient or intuitive on a mobile device. This is because of their experience with social media sites like Facebook and ecommerce sites like Amazon. (Source: Ironpaper)

What can we conclude from these two sets of data? First, your prospects that are going online have questions and they are seeking answers. They are looking for a company they can trust. They want to get a fair value for the money they spend. The majority of them are using the convenience of their mobile device to search for you. They expect to be able to see your site quickly, and scan through it rapidly.

Given those trends, how does your website meet your prospects needs? In many cases it can't. *A traditional website is an electronic brochure, it is designed to be read. A profit funnel is designed to give your prospects opportunities to take action and become customers.*

I understand that you have a website that has been "mobile optimized." Almost all active sites have taken advantage of a plug-in or widget that is added to the site that compresses the text to format on a mobile device. How much does that impact the load speed of your site? Does the resulting compression just jam a lot of text into a narrower display? How does the viewer navigate to other pages on your site given this configuration? "Mobile Optimized" met the standard during the transition period from most users working on a desktop computer to now using their mobile devices. But that was several years ago and the standard has changed. To be competitive your website must be designed to display across a variety of screen sizes and two primary platforms, iPhone and Android.

I want to share the five steps of what we refer to as the "Profit Funnel Formula," and describe each of them. After that I'll share the most current technology designed to meet the needs of today's consumers implementing this formula. The five steps are:

- Lead Magnet
- Trust Trigger

- Core Offering
- Profit Bump
- Funnel Stack

A **Lead Magnet** should be designed to attract the right customer into your sales funnel. To do this effectively you want to target your marketing to a specific group of prospective customers, identify a major problem they are searching for a solution to, and then generate leads with a lead magnet.

Here are some examples of putting this idea into practice. You are an attorney that specializes in trust and estate work. You know from experience talking with past clients that many people are not sure if a trust is the right vehicle to use in protecting or transferring wealth. An effective lead magnet in this case would be a short five- or six-page summary sharing what a Trust is and how it is used by families.

Perhaps another part of your practice is helping business owners build a succession plan to define how the business is to be managed when you retire or pass away. Since that is a very different need, you would create a different Lead Magnet and tailor your marketing to this other group of prospects. Maybe in this case you offer a checklist of the ten most important questions a business owner should consider when deciding to sell or transfer their business to heirs.

As a remodeling contractor you specialize in master bath updates. You know that the homeowners who are your primary prospects live in a home that is valued at $500,000 or more with at least 3000 square feet of floor space. It is a simple matter to identify those neighborhoods and develop a series of direct mail pieces to generate interest in your services. Each contact you make with these homeowners directs them to a landing page with images of past jobs and an outline of the steps you take when doing a remodel. You can also accomplish this digitally with a "hyper-local" banner ad campaign.

A veterinarian might develop a list of symptoms that your dog or cat exhibits that might indicate they are ill and make it available by email for anyone who requests it. A dentist can offer free or discounted teeth whitening for potential new patients. Roofing contractors a free "on the roof" inspection with photos of what they find.

The right lead magnet is a free or deeply discounted offer that attracts your ideal customer who exchanges their contact information for your offer. The best lead magnets are either information based or service based. A great lead magnet reveals the problem that your product or service solves! Here are some examples:

- Checklist
- Cheat Sheet
- Reports/Guides
- Trial Offers
- Scripts
- eBooks
- Resource Lists
- Personal Assessment Sample
- Audit Report
- Insider Research
- Micro-Service

One reason lead magnets are so powerful is that they are working for you 24/7, attracting more leads and pre-selling them into new customers.

Prospects are more likely to become customers, and spend more money with your company, when they trust you. That's why developing a **Trust Trigger** is an integral component in your profit funnel. A trust trigger is a lower priced offer that over delivers in value as a way of developing trust and authority for you and your business so that you can more easily move the prospect to your core offer.

A trust trigger might be as inexpensive as $20, or much more depending on the value of your core offer. The goal is to help your prospect spend money in an initial interaction with you and to "trigger" the trust needed to buy your more expensive core offer almost immediately.

Let me share an example from our business. One of our Core 5® services we offer clients is reputation marketing. That service is priced in a range between $500 and $1,200 each month, depending on a variety of factors. A trust trigger that we use to introduce this service is called "5 Stars in 5 Days."

To implement this Trust Trigger we get a list of fifty or more past customers from our prospect. Then we enter those customers into one of our autoresponders, connected to a webpage we build that has been branded to match the look of our prospects website. We send their customers two emails inviting them to leave a review of their experience with the company and make it easy for them to publish their review online. We charge as little as $27 for this as a way of introducing our reputation programs.

At the end of the five days we go back to the prospect, show them the new reviews that have been generated by this initial effort, and invite them to our "core offer" of a full reputation marketing service.

Your **Core Offer** is the primary product or service that you want to sell to a specific group of prospects. It is one of the central services you offer and where you should be making most of your revenue and profit. Your core offer could be a one-time sale, monthly or quarterly residual service, or both.

If done correctly, your lead magnet and trust trigger should do a great job of educating, preselling, and building the trust and authority that is needed for you to sell your core offer.

The **Profit Bump** is a one-time offer upsell that enhances or maximizes the benefits of your core offer. This is where you can dramatically increase your client acquisition profits. This upsell can be a one-time offer or monthly subscription. Some ways that we've seen companies implement this is with a "level up bump." This is an upgraded enhancement to your core offer that is a 'must have' if they want to maximize the value of the core offer.

If you've ever purchased a new automobile you've experience several 'level up bumps' when the salesperson offers the 'special undercoat' or a 'spray in bed liner' for your new truck. Amazon does this when you buy a book. Notice the offer near the bottom of the screen when you choose a book. It will usually have a headline like, "Customers who purchased this book also bought..." and there will be two other books by the same author or on the same subject. Then they'll offer all three for a "special price." Ever purchased computer, television, or other electronics? Remember the offer for a 'service contract?' That was a level up bump.

Another profit bump strategy is the "VIP Bump." This is an additional high dollar 'Rockstar' status offer that gives your customers VIP treatment and allows exclusive access and treatments with your products or services.

We worked with a chiropractor who implemented this strategy. For a monthly fee the patient could come in for an unlimited number of adjustments each week. They could make an appointment or just drop in. The office had several chiropractors, so the members of this VIP group would be adjusted by the next available doctor. They had an advanced patient management software program and computer monitors mounted on the wall in each service room. Even if the doctor had never treated a patient before, when he or she walked into the room they could quickly review the entire patient record on the screen and know exactly how to treat that individual. On the surface it would seem that this plan would be a money loser with patients showing up every day for an adjustment. In practice it guaranteed a monthly cash flow for the practice, and very few patients came in more than once or twice a week.

Another example of the VIP Bump is the "Safety Club." This works especially well for certain contractors. It means that your customer pays an annual fee to belong to the Safety Club. You offer a series of benefits all designed to help a homeowner rest easy knowing that a professional is monitoring an important part of their home. Example that we've implemented for clients include the 'Overhead Safety

Club' for roofing customers, 'Garage Door Safety Club' or 'Furnace and Air Conditioning Safety Club."

We offer a similar "VIP Bump" to our clients with our "Total Market Takeover®" program. This is where we bundle all our services, both on and offline, and focus them on behalf of a single client in a market niche and city. In return for a client engaging us at this level we commit to only working with them in their area. For a dentist in Austin, they are guaranteed to be the only dentist in Austin that we work with. A roofing contractor in Jacksonville, same thing, we will not take on another roofer in Jacksonville. This has been a mutually beneficial relationship with a select few clients that we offer it to.

The final step, a **Funnel Stack** is where you create a new offer that you present after the profit bump. This offer follows the same four step pattern I've just described. You might offer right after the initial sale or wait several days or even a month before making the offer. This is especially effective for companies that have several unique products that will benefit a customer.

There is one more step to a well-designed profit funnel I want to share. That is the "Re-offer Campaign." The reality is that not every prospect will purchase every offer in your funnel. This creates a huge opportunity to go back to your non-buyers and "re-offer" them the products or services they didn't buy the first time going through your funnel.

Because they have already entered your funnel you know them and do not have the initial cost of acquiring the customer through your lead magnet. This means the profit on a re-offer campaign will be higher than any other profit you create. The best part about a re-offer campaign is that it can be automated with email, voicemail, and SMS follow ups to do all the work.

If all of this sounds complicated and a little intimidating, well, it can be. To make things more difficult, these steps cannot be accomplished with a traditional website. How do you tell your story with a logical beginning, middle, and end on a 10+ page website? You can't, especially for the prospects searching from their mobile device. Here's another point: how can you split test your content on a 10+ page website? You can't. The two most important things you need to do to make your web pages convert prospects into customers are not possible with your website.

What's the answer? A Funnel Site. This new technology was introduced in early 2019 and offers the solution to the challenges I've suggested in the previous pages. A funnel site is designed to move the visitor into the sales process. It tells your company story with a beginning, middle, and end that helps the visitor make the decision to choose you.

First, let me compare and contrast a funnel site with the more traditional site that most us have used for years. Your website is a horizontal design with multiple pages, each focused on some aspect of your company. It is more challenging to navigate, particularly from a mobile phone. It is unusual to have clear action steps or calls to action other than a "Contact Us" page. It is not possible to split test copy or graphics to test effectiveness. Tracking conversions is also difficult.

A funnel site is all built on a single page or vertical orientation with user friendly scrolling navigation. Rather than being "mobile friendly" the code used to develop the funnel site software was actually designed for mobile. It also displays well on a desktop but was specifically coded for mobile phones and tablets. Since the entire site is a single page, it is easy to replicate the page and change one or two elements for accurate split testing. Each site can be built with six to ten calls to action and feature your lead magnets. These specific calls to action make it easy to track conversions and the level of visitor interest in specific offers. Adding video is easy. All the search engine optimization strategies that are built into a more traditional site are also found on a funnel website.

If you'd like to see an example of a funnel website, please visit ours: thealchemyconsultinggroup.com.

The key to the readability of funnel sites is that are built using "story blocks." There are 19 unique blocks, each designed for a specific purpose. When we customize a site for a client the organizational structure might look like this (some of the blocks are repeated in this example of an actual site that we built):

- Title/Navigation Block
- Cover Block
- Our Promise Block
- Services; 6 to 8 Services
- Call to Action Block
- Testimonial #1 Block
- Offer Block

- Featured Service #1
- Featured Service #2
- Featured Service #3
- Case Study, Project Portfolio Block
- Contact Us Banner Block
- Myth Block
- Who We Are Block
- Our Expertise Block
- Our Team Block
- 2nd Testimonial Block
- Call Us Today Block
- FAQ Block
- Map Address and Hours Block
- Footer

Of course that is just an example of the flow of a site. Every site is different depending on the needs of the client and the products/services being offered. This formula is the starting point of building your company story and gives us the foundation to start split testing to increase your website conversions.

The 21-step structure that I've just shared is what we would call a Brand Site Funnel. It is similar to the website that you may have now in that it is designed to tell your company story while offering the visitor multiple ways to interact with you.

An alternative is a Lead Generation funnel. This format is a shorter site that will feature the lead magnet you have chosen, a way for the prospect to opt in and get the lead magnet, a thank you page, and one or more landing pages as needed to bring prospects into your funnel. There will also be a three to five step email follow up, with each email directing the reader to another information or landing page. A Lead Gen funnel takes the prospect through the five steps I described earlier.

If you are doing any type of paid advertising, Google PPC or Banner Campaigns, having one or more landing pages is critical to the success of the campaign. These are easily created using the story block structure. Here again the ability to easily set up A/B split tests to continue to refine your marketing message is a distinct advantage.

One additional point to recommend a funnel site. They are generally less expensive to build than a traditional website, and much easier to update with fresh content, images, and video.

The dynamic nature of the Internet, and the pace of change, mandate that business owners continue to innovate if they want to stay ahead of the competition. The increasing dominance of mobile based search in the last eighteen months is going to give companies that make it easy for their prospects to get information and make a decision a clear market edge. Building a funnel that creates trust in you and your services and allows a prospect to proceed at a pace comfortable for them, will help you gain market share.

"Entrepreneurism is just problem solving for money."

--Michael Hyatt

Reputation Marketing--Your Business is "In the Stars"

It is not an exaggeration to say that controlling and marketing your reputation online has become the single most critical aspect of any online marketing you do for your company. This task is completely different from the Search Engine Optimization or Social Media Marketing that is the mainstream, and that you have a lot of companies calling every week and offering to do for you. The reality is that the strategy for online marketing of your business forever changed in September of 2014.

Did you know that?

I know, 2014 is "ancient history" in the world of the Internet, but it's important that you understand just how significant this change was, and how it is still impacting search results. Let me take just a paragraph and describe the changes. In August 2014 the search engines dramatically changed their algorithm for ranking websites on their search result pages. This wasn't just Google; Bing and Yahoo agreed and rewrote their programs at the same time. Here is the major change. Prior to that time where your site appeared on the page was the result of a complicated calculation that included more than

200 variables but was most heavily weighted by the number of "backlinks" connected to your site. Without going into a lot of tech-speak let me say that it was a relatively simple matter for those of us in the Search Engine Optimization business to artificially manufacture these backlinks. Which meant that we could take a website and drive it to the first pages of the search engines using technology without regard to how many people might actually be looking for or finding value on the website.

The fundamental change that was implemented is replacing backlinks as a primary criterion for page rank with your company reputation, as defined by actual customers who have used your service and then posted a review of their experience online. The search engines are now sending their spiders through dozens of "review sites" looking for comments about your company. When they find one, it is harvested and combined with other reviews in a formula that results in a "Star Rating" for your business. One star is bad, five stars is the best.

This is a game changer in how you market your company online. In this chapter I want to share with you what you can do to take advantage of the reputation wave. It is a fact that I find amazing, but all these years later many companies still do not have a plan in place to consistently grow their reputation online.

That's good news for you reading this chapter--you can be the market leader in your area. Here's what we're going to talk about:

- Specific game changers and how they impact your business

- What your prospects are looking for today in choosing a business
- What is "Reputation Marketing"
- Strategies to make your company the reputation market leader
- Some questions about Reputation Marketing we often hear

Before I share those ideas with you, let me ask a question. I'm sure you realize that every day people go online searching for a product or service vendor. But do you know just how many people are searching? You might be surprised. At the time I'm writing this, March 2020, I asked one of our support team members to do a quick analysis of how many people searched for a HVAC contractor in several cities around the country. This is the number of people who search *each month*, on average, in each of these cities:

Phoenix, AZ	3118
Miami, FL	3670
Charlotte, NC	1568
Portland, OR	1847
Des Moines, IA	948
Columbus, OH	2983

Just imagine hundreds if not thousands of people online every single month looking for your business. The question is, can they find you? Everyday people in your community are looking for the product or service that you offer. As they do so, they are asking themselves these questions: "who should I do business with? Who can I trust?" What they're doing is looking for the most reputable company. In this chapter I'm going to show you how to make sure that you are the business that they call, and not your competition.

Here's another question for you. Think about your own process when you are looking for a specific product or service. Would you buy from a company that has bad ratings and reviews? Obviously you wouldn't. But let me suggest a more realistic way to think about that question.

Three companies are, for all practical purposes, identical. All three have what you are looking for, and the price point is the same. One has six good reviews; the other has four good reviews but one bad. And the third has no reviews at all. Which one do you buy from? Almost everyone would say the company with six good reviews. Now why is that? Because we want to have a great buying experience too. We're looking to see that a company is consistent in delivering that experience on that product or service that we want to buy.

This is exactly what prospects looking for your company do every single day. They go online and search to find the most reputable company to do business with. Only one bad review can send the customer from your website or your listing online to someone else's. That means the difference between your phone ringing or your competition's phone ringing.

Four Game Changers That Affect Your Company Today

Game Changer Number One. When you do a search for a company name and their city, the resulting listing reveals the company's reputation. Let me say it a different way. Google and the other search engines are going to share the reputation information they have associated with your business listing whether you want them to or not!

Here's why this game changer is so important: anyone searching for a company listing, even just for directions or to get the phone number, is going to see their reputation. This is done automatically by the search engines, as a business you have no control over your reputation being shown.

Consider the situation where someone recommends your company to a friend. According to both Real Strategic and Bright Local there is an 87% probability that the person will look up your company online...maybe just to get the phone number. If you have a poor review score, what are the chances they are going to call you? Even though they were referred, in the past almost a guarantee that you'd get an opportunity to bid for that business, if your reputation score is less than 4 stars they will probably go elsewhere.

Test this for yourself. Take a minute right now, open a browser window and enter your company name and the city you work in. What is your reputation score? Does it show no reviews at all, or some good and others not so good? This is what your prospects see too.

Game Changer Number Two. Customer reviews are now a major factor in almost every type of online marketing, and this is all done automatically. Your reviews, good and bad, show up in your Google My Business listing. (Same for the other search engines.) Your star rating is included in your Pay Per Click ads. They show up on organic website listings. They show up in local directories like Yelp and City Search and Bing and Yahoo, in the online Yellow Pages. Reviews are now a major factor in almost every type of online marketing. Like it or not, everyone searching for your company or in your category will see them.

Which leads us to <u>game changer number three</u>: and that's the reality that Search Engine Optimization, social media, Pay Per Click ads, local marketing--all of the strategies we've done on line for the past five or more years--none of it is as effective anymore if you have bad reviews or a bad reputation online.

I want you to think carefully about what I'm going to write next--especially those of you who have done it yourself or paid someone to do online marketing for you. Maybe you're still paying. *Why would you want to do all that work, spend all the time and money getting to the top of the search engines, and then when people find your business they see bad reviews? You've just wasted your resources!*

At Alchemy Consulting we've totally changed how we prioritize work with our clients. In the past we would do several activities to start. We'd analyze and update the on-page optimization of a website, claim some directory sites, create a blog, write press releases, our tech people would create link wheels all designed to help our clients get to the first page for their primary keywords. That's completely the opposite of what today's marketing is about.

Step one if you want to be effective in marketing online today is you need to create a five-star reputation first. Then market your products and services online. Your phone is not going ring if you don't have the five-star reputation that your prospects are looking for.

What Your Prospects Are Looking for Today in Choosing a Product or Service Provider

OK, let's change it up a little. I've been pretty negative about the impact reputation has made on search results, but there are some really some positive aspects that are a result of this emphasis on reputation.

Game Changer Number Four. Reviews send you prequalified, presold customers; the reason is because buyers trust reviews as much as personal recommendations. That is to say that reviews can be incredibly bad for you if they're bad. But they can be incredibly good for you if they're good! According to independent studies conducted by two international marketing agencies, Bright Local and Local Marketing Genius, 87% of people who are referred to a business will first go online and look up the company's reputation. That is almost 9 out of every 10 prospects!

Now, stop for a minute and think about growing your company. Would you rather create a marketing plan that focused on people that don't know you, don't like you, don't trust you, and always are worried about price? Or would you prefer a marketing plan that attracts people that feel they know you, people that already like you, people that trust you and act like they are all referrals?

Of course you want the latter, you want to create a referral-based marketing plan. Well, for the first time ever our online marketing can be just as powerful as referral marketing. Why, because nine out of ten people trust reviews just as much as personal recommendations!

That means you need those five-star reviews on your website and on your listings. That's as good as someone's mother saying you should shop at this company. That's as good as someone's best friend saying, you know what, you should call ABC Plumbing, I used them, and they were amazing. Having positive reviews is just as good as a colleague at work saying look, if you need a new roof you should go to this business. They do a great job. You can think of it that way because eighty seven percent of buyers trust reviews just as much as personal recommendations.

Reviews are powerful marketing that you need for your business.

If you're not yet convinced why having a 5-star reputation is so vital to business let me share just one more statistic with you. Consumers look up an average of 10 reviews before making a decision. What does this mean for your business? First, all these consumers are online. They're looking for reviews. Second, and more important, they're looking at multiple reviews, not just one or two.

For those of you that have been wondering to yourself how many reviews is enough, here's your answer. Seventy-eight percent of consumers trust a business with a minimum of 6-10 reviews. That means you want a minimum of ten 5-star reviews for your business.

That's the current statistic, but here's the advice I give our clients. Let's see how many reviews your primary competitors have. If one of them has 35 reviews, then you need 40. However, from the perspective of the search engines, it isn't just the number of reviews that is important. They also calculate the "recency" in their algorithm and give reviews less than 90 days old a much higher score than those that are more dated

The reality of the marketplace today is that you are not credible without five-star reviews. Without a five-star reputation and a minimum of ten recent reviews, your business just can't be trusted when people find you. This is the difference between your phone ringing and it not ringing. More importantly, this the difference between your phone not ringing and your competition's phone ringing.

What exactly is Reputation Marketing?

It's simple. Reputation Marketing is positioning your company as the market leader in front of thousands of buyers with your five-star reputation. It's building a five-star reputation online <u>and</u> <u>then going out and marketing that reputation</u>. As we just learned, this is the most powerful and trusted type of marketing you can do to grow your company in today's market.

OK, enough background…let's get to the bottom line. How do you create a reputation marketing program for your business? Here is a step-by-step strategy.

What is your online reputation today?

The first step is to really understand your current reputation. So let me ask you. Do you know you reputation online? Do you know what people are saying about you right now? If you didn't do it a few minutes ago when I suggested, then take a minute right now and go online, type in your business name and city, not with the www, just your business name. Click enter.

The results page will start with your paid ads if you are using Google AdWords in your marketing. Then in most cases you'll see a link to your website followed by several links to individual pages within your website.

What I want you to look at is on the right side of the page where Google offers a more complete listing of your business. This is your "Google My Business" listing. If you have properly claimed this listing it will include photos you have uploaded as well as accurate information on your business hours and address. There will also be a link someone can click on to go to your website and another link to get directions to your place of business.

Most important, right under your business name, is a summary of your review star rating and a clickable link so someone can go read those reviews.

What did you find? Do you have current reviews (less than 90 days old) for prospects to read? If not then you are losing business opportunities.

Now do a more general search for one of the important keywords for your business and your city. For example, if you own a massage spa in Orlando, type in "massage spa Orlando" or "massage therapy Orlando" or "couples massage Orlando" or another primary keyword you want to rank for. Several of your competitors will be on the first page. Many search categories also have what we call the "map pack" of three or four listings that are highlighted and separate from the organic listings.

As a general rule, the companies in this Map Pack are leaders in the category and will have quite a few reviews. I occasionally see exceptions, or a company with more reviews than one in the Map Pack but is elsewhere on page one or two. Buried somewhere in Google's algorithm is a reason for this apparent discrepancy. What is important is not to focus on the infrequent anomaly, but to concentrate on enhancing your company's reputation.

Reputation Rules Update

There are three other "rules" that the search engines consider in the credibility of reviews. These have been enacted more recently.

1. All reviews must have a minimum of 30 characters or they will not be included in your star rating calculation. The search engines are looking for a couple of sentences from your customers describing their experience. Giving a five-star rating with no comment, or just a couple of words is no longer acceptable.

2. Reviews older than 24 months will no longer be considered. This means that every month all reviews that are two years old "drop out" of your star rating. Google wants to be sure that your prospects are seeing reviews that reflect your current level of service.

3. Companies with a new star rating of less than 4.0 will be penalized in search results. That means that your website will not be presented to someone searching for a vendor in your business category as frequently if your net score is not at least 4.0.

To put that in perspective, the average star rating for all companies in all   business niches in the United States is

4.16. In essence, Google is asking that you are "almost average" to maintain your status in the search engine results pages. If your rating is less than 4.0 it doesn't mean your site will not be offered when a prospect is searching for a contractor, but it will not be shown as frequently.

4. "Anonymous" reviews will no longer be posted. That is, reviews from "a Google user" that used to be allowed have now been deleted by the Google. Every review must be 'signed' by the reviewer.

Building Your 5-Star Reputation

I hope that I have conveyed the importance of achieving an excellent online reputation as defined by your Star Rating with the search engines. If you have never focused on developing your online reputation, how do you do it? Here are some steps to consider:

First, your staff needs to be made aware of the important role each of them play in building your company reputation. You will want to create a reputation marketing culture in your company. It's not enough to try to fix things after the fact, you want to be proactive inside your business to make sure that every single person in your company is on the same page when it comes to service standards.

Ongoing management of your reputation is not a "one and done" process, you want to continue to keep your 5-star reputation going. In reality you're only one customer away from a bad review. Think about it, everybody has a bad day: the receptionist, your salesperson, one of the guys out on a crew, even you. Every one of our businesses is just one day and just one customer away from a bad review. We want to keep every team member's eyes on the ball to make sure we stay focused.

Second, where do you want your reviews to be found? There are literally hundreds of sites where a customer can leave a comment about your company, how do you prioritize them? Simple, just one word: Google.

For almost every business in every niche the most important place to ask a customer to leave a review is on your Google My Business page. This is where prospects will be searching, make it easy for them to find you.

There are exceptions. Restaurants are best served building their reputation on Yelp and hospitality industry companies on Trip Advisor. We have a massage therapy client who has built a nice segment of her business with people vacationing from out of town and looking to get a massage by have a great rating with Trip Advisor. Medical practices can choose from a wide variety of specialty sites, but I still recommend Google since most of their prospective patients won't know to look on these sites.

If you have not yet "claimed" your Google My Business page make this a high priority. Go to this link and click the "Start Now" button: business.google.com.

Third, make it easy for your customers to leave a review. We like to provide our clients with a simple business card that has an invitation to leave a review and gives them the link they'll need to get to your Google My Business or other location where you would like them to review you.

The best time to invite someone to leave a review is at the end of the transaction. If you wait just a couple of days and send them an email invitation the percentage of people who will follow through and leave a review drops significantly.

By handing them a card with directions, personally asking for a positive review, and sharing how important this is for your business, many people will take the time to leave a review.

Fourth, consider a third-party review collection and display program. Did you know there are several software programs that have been developed specifically to request and post reviews? These are usually available only through advertising agencies or search engine optimization companies. If you have a marketing company working on your behalf, ask them about this.

We use one of these programs for our clients and have found that automating this process on their behalf saves the business owner a lot of time and results in more reviews being given. We also monitor 15 of the most common Internet directories where someone can leave a review so that our clients can quickly respond to both good and not-so-good reviews.

If you decide to employ an agency to help you develop and maintain your online reputation be sure they are compliant with the latest Google updates I mentioned earlier.

Many of these software programs offer an "internal loop" that divert a negative review, generally defined as 3 stars or less, to a different page that did not allow the reviewer to forward their review to the internet. Instead, it 'captured' that review and sent it to the business owner for their response. *This strategy has been specifically prohibited by the new search engine guidelines.* Do not make the mistake of engaging one of these services, you could see your website severely penalized.

Fifth, the testimonials you have on your website are not included in your overall star rating by the search engines. In fact, they are not indexed at all. Since they cannot be sourced to an IP address that is independent from your website, the search engine spiders ignore them completely.

Related to this is an important fact. Frequently I'll be asked, "why can't I just have several of my employees type these old testimonials into the Google page and have them used?" The simple answer is that Google tracks the individual computer address (its IP address) that is the source of the review. If multiple reviews are submitted for the same company from that unique address they will all be ignored. (If you have a company server and multiple computers in your office, Google views this as one IP address connected to your server. Don't try it.)

How can you include your good reviews on your website? Several of the third-party review programs have a way to add their review collection page to your website. Your web master can add an item into the menu bar for reviews and paste the code for the review page into your site. One of the reasons we use the program we do for our clients is the ease of doing this.

Sixth, you'll also want to post your 5-star reviews on the social media sites you belong to. With all of the talk about social media in the last couple of years, for many companies it has been a disappointment as far as generating new business. That all changes when you're using reputation marketing in your social media. When 5-star reviews are being posted several times each week to your Facebook, Instagram, LinkedIn and other pages they become a powerful source of leads.

Seven, do you have salespeople in your company? It doesn't matter if they work on site or off, when you arm them with marketing pieces featuring your 5-star reviews their closing rates will go up dramatically. Imagine the ability to sit in front of a prospect that's on the fence about whether they should go with you or buy from a competitor. Then you say, "don't take my word for it. Let's go online and see what other customers just like you experienced, and what they thought about working with us." Then you read all your five-star reviews in front of them.

You should also provide each salesperson with a hard copy of the reviews in a notebook to show a prospect that might not have a computer handy. You can also use an iPad or Android pad, as most people will have wireless in their homes. Remember, statistically speaking, having those reviews is just as powerful as having their best friend or family member, a colleague at work recommending your company to that customer. You're going to be able to close a lot more sales if you arm yourself with reputation marketing.

Some Questions About Reputation Marketing

One that comes up a lot. "I have had someone leave a bad review on Yelp, how can I delete it?"

The short answer is that you can't. I know that there are companies out there who promise to eliminate past bad reviews, but the truth is it's just not possible. The only real solution is to focus on generating as many 4- and 5-star reviews as you can, as quickly as possible. Most all the sites display reviews in order of most recent first. Over a period of a few months you will be able to "push down" the bad review so not as many people see it.

There is also an "aging" component to the calculation used to determine your star rating. The most recent reviews are given a greater emphasis by the review sites that aggregate reviews and apply a rating number.

The only exception to this is your Facebook business page. If someone says something negative there, you or your page administrator can delete the conversation. The challenge is that you must monitor Facebook frequently so you can stop a problem review before it goes viral.

Another question we frequently hear is from businesses with multiple locations. "How do the search engines determine the reputation of our company if we're in several towns or have more than one office in our city?" Here's the reality if you have multiple offices. While it's the same company, it is multiple locations to the search engines and the prospects looking for a vendor in each city. That means you need to do all the work of claiming your listing on the review sites and building your places page for each of the search engines for every location. If you have offices in three cities, you'll need three places pages and to claim the top dozen or sites at a minimum for each location.

One more question has to do with the weather. Many contractors who can only work outside six to eight months a year run another business in the winter. How should they handle reputation marketing? If your "winter" business uses a different name and is a completely different business from your "summer" company, then you'll need to do all the steps I've described for that business as well. If you do landscape in the summer but remodel kitchens in the winter, and use the same business name for both activities, you only need to claim your sites one time.

Keep in mind that most of the review sites use your primary business telephone number as their method of identifying your company. If you do run both businesses using the same main number, you'll want to talk about the two companies in the description section of the listings you claim.

This has been a lot of information but is possibly the most important information I can share with you to help your business grow. The online reputation of your company is critical to your success. I encourage you to implement these steps as soon as you can.

My nomination for the greatest entrepreneur in history: Christopher Columbus.

He left home not knowing where he was going.
He arrived not knowing where he landed,
He went home not knowing where he'd been,
He did it all on borrowed money!

--Anonymous

Paid Traffic—The Fastest Path to Page One

A consistent flow of new prospects is the lifeblood of your business. Whether it is people walking into your shop or office, or finding you online, without this "traffic" your business will not survive for very long. Every time I have met with a business owner it doesn't take long for the conversation to turn to the acquisition of new customers.

There are two primary Internet based ways to help prospects find your business: organic search and paid traffic. I share ideas for enhancing your organic search results in the chapter "Getting Found Online." In this chapter I want to focus on the other channel: paid traffic.

Here again you will find two primary methods for driving traffic to your business. They are Google Adwords (other search engines also offer paid advertising, but Google controls so much of this market that for simplicity sake I will just refer to this category of advertising as (Google AdWords.") You will often hear people describe this category of advertising as "Pay Per Click" or "PPC" for short.

When you do a Google search almost all the time at the top of the first page of the search results will be three or four paid ads. You'll be able to recognize that the business has paid for these by the designation "Ad" next to the text. As a general rule, any listing you find above the box with the map is a paid ad. More recently you will see in some business niches a series of company listings above the paid ads that are "Google Guaranteed" companies. These are listings for companies that have gone through a process of being qualified by Google and that pay a fee for this level of approval from Google.

The other category of paid advertising is Real Time Bidding, more frequently referred to as Banner Advertising. A banner campaign might be "re-targeting" people who have visited your website or cold marketing banner ads based on demographic or geographic specifications. You can also employ a strategy called "hyper-local" and pinpoint prospects within a very close proximity to your place of business or even your booth at a trade show. You may have heard the term "geo-fencing" to describe this type of campaign.

For most companies or practices in almost every category the best opportunity you have to quickly attract new prospects is through paid advertising. As I share in the Getting Found Online chapter, it is no longer realistic to depend on organic search results, especially for a newer business. The good news is that paid advertising programs that were financially untenable for a local business just two years ago can now be implemented with a very affordable monthly investment.

In the next few pages I'm going to give you an overview of both PPC and Banner Advertising. My purpose is to introduce you to these channels and give you enough information to ask the right questions as you consider working with someone to help you manage a campaign or design and manage your own. If you do an Amazon search for books on "PPC" you'll find that there 12 books available with that keyword. I know because I just did it...now for the next couple of days I'll see banner ads offering me these books...because Amazon is a master at Re-Targeting.

You are probably more familiar with Google Adwords, so let's start there.

A PPC advertising program is quite simple to begin. You create an account with the search engines, an "Adwords" account as Google names it. Your account is funded with a credit card. Then you place an advertisement that is tied to the keywords that you believe your prospects will search. Every time your ad is clicked, sending a visitor to your website or a landing page, you pay the search engine a small fee. When PPC is working correctly, the fee is trivial, because *the visit is worth more than what you pay for it*. In other words, if we pay $36 for a click, but the click results in a $1,000 sale, then you've made a hefty profit. Of course not all clicks result in a customer, and not all customers spend the same amount with you.

Do you remember my discussion in the opening chapter of this book about average transaction value and lifetime customer value? Knowing these numbers for your business is critical if you want to have a successful paid advertising campaign.

How is the value of a "click" determined? It's an open, and very competitive, marketplace. You bid the amount you are willing to spend for click on a particular keyword. This requires careful research before you launch your campaign. A personal injury attorney in Los Angeles would expect to pay $175 or more for each click on his or her ad. That same ad in another market, Jackson, Mississippi for example, might only cost $27. There is a common misconception that the ad listed first must be paying more for click traffic than the ads below. This is not true. Ad placement, and your individual cost per click, are based on your "quality score" as determined by the search engine. More on this later.

First, why would a business owner invest in paid advertising, particularly in a wide open and potentially expensive marketplace like Adwords? There are quite a few good reasons. Consider:

Generate new leads: Use PPC to obtain new prospects and gather information about their needs over time. You can drive new prospects to a special landing page where they can sign up for a free demo or download a new report or free content.

Direct Sales: Drive new leads to a transaction or sales page

Build Brand Awareness: Use PPC to invite prospects to an event, either on or offline, or to promote something newsworthy.

Pay for Performance: You only pay for actual clicks to your listing. If a user enters a search term, sees your site and clicks the listing, it is because s/he believes your listing will provide the info s/he wants.

Control what visitors see on your site; focus the conversation: You can direct traffic to specific pages on your site. You should develop landing pages for each campaign, pages offering specific information and a strong call to action. These are separate from your primary website.

Excellent timing: You bid on the search terms/keywords used by your prospects when they are searching for info about what you offer on the web.

Bid what a prospect is worth: You can input different bid amounts on keywords to reflect how valuable the leads are for you. For example, you may bid on a very specific phrase such as, "Roofing Contractor, Portland," and pay more for those clicks because they are more valuable to you than general keywords that may drive a greater volume of less targeted traffic.

Limit Your Spending: You can choose a maximum bid level for each click, as well as a total spend you are willing to make each day. This way you only spend what those website visits are worth to you.

Speed to market: You can launch a paid search campaign as soon as your website is live, building immediate traffic that may take months to generate organically.

Develop Targeted Campaigns: You can develop very specific campaigns that include seasonality, regionality, and other factors that influence the purchasing decision.

Who is Google's Customer?

Another important question to consider when building a paid ad campaign is, "who is Google's customer?" At first glance you might assume it is the company that is buying advertising, since that is Google's primary source of revenue. That would be wrong. Google considers their customer to be the person entering the search term into their browser and trying to find information. Even if you're spending $100K a month on Adwords, and many companies do, that still doesn't make that business more important than the searcher.

Knowing that, how does it impact the way you structure your ad campaigns? You want to make it easy for the searcher to find exactly what they're looking for (what they 'clicked' for) when they choose your ad. Frequently this means taking them to a landing page that is focused on the exact topic that your ad is. Here's an example:

Let's say you're a plumbing contractor that offers 24-hour emergency service. One of your trucks in on call every night, and you have a special phone number that goes to a mobile phone for whomever is on call that night. Mrs. Smith has a plumbing emergency at 2 am, so goes online to find an emergency plumber. She sees your paid ad, "24-Hour Emergency Plumber" at the top of the page and clicks on it. She then finds herself on the home page of your website. There she can learn that you've been in business for 27 years, have a friendly staff and see a picture of one of your trucks. However, there is nothing about how to contact the 24-hour emergency service.

Within seconds Mrs. Smith clicks off your site and goes to the next paid ad offering emergency service. When she clicks on it, she is taken to a landing page that has, in large bold type, "24-HOUR EMERGENCIES, CALL 555-555-1212. That number might even be set as a "click to call" number so if she is on her mobile phone she can just touch it and immediately dial your number. Having found her answer, Mrs. Smith makes the call and stops searching.

Think about how Google views that transaction. They track the keywords Mrs. Smith entered, and offer her a page that is most congruent with those search terms. Then the Google bot records the fact that Mrs. Smith clicked on your ad, but within seconds left and came back to her search. That tells Google she did not find what she wanted on your site...bad for you! On her next search she not only stayed longer on the page she selected but stopped searching after that page...good for your competitor!

There are a couple of lessons to take from this simple example. First, Mrs. Smith finding what she needs, and quickly, is Googles top priority. Second, if your ad is for a specific product or service make sure than when a prospect clicks on the ad they can find information on that specific product or service right away. People are impatient, if they have to look for something they won't. If the Internet has subconsciously trained us about anything it is that we can always find what we want if we keep clicking.

Your Quality Score

The other fact that is buried in this example, that will cost or make you money, is the concept of your Quality Score with

Google. The placement of your ad on the page for each keyword that you are targeting is determined by your Quality Score. This score is determined by the search engines using a complicated algorithm that is frequently updated and considered a 'trade secret.'

However, as Google Certified ad managers we know most of the basics. In brief, here's how the formula works. Where your ad appears on the page (your "ad rank") is determined by your maximum bid amount for that keyword times your Quality Score. The cost of your ad if it is selected by the searcher is calculated as: The Ad Rank of the advertisement below you divided by your Quality Score plus a penny.

That's probably more than you wanted to know. The more important question is, "how can I influence and improve my Quality Score?" Ahh, if only it were that simple! Google actually has seven different types of quality scores: account level, ad group, keyword level, ad level, landing page, display network, and mobile. These seven categories comprise the different components that go into building a properly designed and managed Adwords campaign. If you want to implement PPC advertising for your company there are quite a few online sources you can get guides to help with this. All of these will discuss the importance of quality score and how to enhance it. The level of detail to describe strategies for each of the seven types of quality scores is beyond the scope of this book, but if you decide to start with PPC please do research or hire an experienced agency before pulling out your credit card.

Building a Good PPC Ad

That being said, I would be remiss if I didn't offer you some tips on designing a proper ad, one that will give you the best opportunity to attract clicks while enhancing your quality score. Here are five important considerations when it comes to developing a successful PPC ad:

Competitive Research. What do other companies in your business niche say in their ads? Take some time and do this exercise: Identify the top ten keywords you'd like to rank for and type each of them into the browser. Then take a screenshot of the paid ads and print them out so you can more easily study them. What is the headline of the ad? Many times a company will just use their name. This is a mistake. Unless the company has spent a lot of money and time with radio or television advertising the average consumer will probably not recognize their company name. It is not uncommon to include terms like, "best plumber in town" or something equally trite. Searchers do not believe these meaningless platitudes, don't use them!

To be effective you want your ad to have a powerful headline. We worked with a roofing company several years ago that use the slogan, "think you need a new roof—think again." We tested that in several PPC campaigns with great success. The point is, be different and you will get more clicks.

Identify Differentiating Characteristics. Now that you've assessed the competition, use your knowledge to become the leader of the pack. Consider your page-mates ad copy and identify a differentiator that will make you stand out. This is your opportunity to sell yourself! Tell the searcher why you are providing them a better product or deal than your competitors.

Maybe it's your years in the marketplace, or top ranking from the BBB, or your company was selected for an industry award. Anything that might attract attention and prompt a Searcher to read your ad.

Include A Call to Action. To complete your ad, include a call to action that gives your searchers an incentive to click. You can opt for the standard "call us now," but if you really want to step it up a notch, consider a more creative alternative. If you have a high profile past client (and get their permission) say something like "Coach Smith trusted his home air conditioner to us, you should too." Make an offer that gives something of value to a homeowner: "Free evaluation of your case" as an example for a law office.

Use Ad Extensions. Extensions are a way to increase the size of your ad at no additional cost. There are several types of extensions you can utilize. Among them are call extensions, sitelink extensions, location extensions, offer extensions, and application extensions (for people using a tablet or mobile phone to search.)

Watch Your Metrics. Your ad may be complete, but you're not finished yet. Let it get a few impressions and then assess your success! It's tough to predict the performance of a new ad, so ad copy testing is critical. Often the ad copy you thought would win out ends up losing. There's no way to know what will work until you test ads against each other and let prospects inform your decision.

Why Do I Need Landing Pages?

The classic mistake that too many business owners make when starting a new PPC campaign is sending someone who clicks on their ad directly to their website, usually to the home page. "What's wrong with that," you're asking? While you may have an award-winning homepage that was designed by a well-known internet guru who charged you a lot of money, but it may not be at all relevant to the reason someone is searching for you.

Your PPC ad is written for a specific response. It is crafted to speak to a specific need in mind of the Searcher. Your website is a more general introduction to your company and all its products/services. It may not immediately speak to the need in the mind of the prospect. A landing page is a "single page website" that does.

Why does someone need what you offer? What, specifically, are they looking for when they go to a search engine and type in their keywords? That is the question you want to answer for them immediately when they click on your ad.

The way you do this is with a Landing Page. A Landing Page is just what it sounds like, an online page that specifically addresses the exact question the searcher is asking. Remember the 24-hour emergency plumbing example I gave earlier? It was the landing page that provided the immediate answer to Mrs. Smith's concern that won the business.

We call this strategy **"One Decision Marketing"** because it is focused on helping a prospect make the one decision that is most relevant to them at that time. This will also augment your quality score as Google sees searchers finding what they want when clicking your ads.

When I explain this to prospects and clients a common question is, "does that mean I need a landing page for each ad I run?" No, not each individual ad, but a landing page for each product or service you are marketing. You may have several ads, each ad has specific keywords and therefore a specific want or need that it is addressing but are all focused on bringing prospects to a particular product or service. These ads should all be directed to a specific landing page so that a prospective customer has their immediate questions answered.

Let me offer a different example to be sure I'm clear on this important point. As a plastic surgeon you offer a variety of procedures. Tummy tuck, facelift, breast augmentation, mommy makeover, Botox injections, etc. . Each of these areas of specialization might have three or five or even more keyword phrases that are commonly typed in by Searchers. Each of those keyword phrases can have one or more specific ads ("more" because you are constantly testing to improve your results). All of the ads for 'tummy tuck' will link to one landing page that has relevant information to that specific specialty of your practice, and a clear call to action so the Searcher knows exactly what you want them to do next. All of the facelift ads will link to a landing page that only talks about that service.

Does it Make Sense to Outsource PPC Campaigns?

Managing a PPC program with multiple campaigns and ad groups takes both time and expertise. It is a specialized enough task that many business owners choose to outsource their Pay Per Click marketing. If that is something you want to explore then let me give you some tips for finding the right company.

1. Make certain that the firm you retain is actually doing the work. Frequently larger ad agencies will sub-contract paid ad campaigns to someone else and mark up the cost. Another technique I've seen is agencies will "macro-manage" campaigns. What that means is they group together like companies, all dentists or all HVAC contractors for example, and make generic updates to ads for the group rather than analyzing the specific results for your company.
2. Get monthly reports that you can understand. At a minimum you should receive updates on cost, number of impressions, cost per click, click through rate, cost per conversion, and conversion rate. If you are including Click-to-Call ads then a summary of the number of calls and how long they lasted should be analyzed as well.
3. Before accepting you as a client, a good ad manager will ask you specific questions about your ideal prospect, what is your company value proposition, what times of the day/month/year are you the most busy, what is the transaction value of a new customer, lifetime value of that customer, what are you willing to pay to acquire a new customer?
4. The ad manager should also help you analyze what is a realistic budget to meet your goals?

I said earlier that PPC advertising can be an extremely powerful and cost-effective traffic source if managed correctly. Like so many things in our businesses it is that "managed correctly" that is the difference between success and failure.

I want to switch my focus to the other category of creating traffic for your business: Banner advertising. I'm excited to share this with you because it is a strategy that has only recently become affordable for a local business. It is still largely unknown, which means that the business owner who implements now will have a significant advantage over the competition.

Banner Advertising for Consistent Traffic

Have you ever shopped on Amazon? Or more recently eBay? Even if you didn't buy anything you've experienced one category of Banner Advertising: Re-targeting. That is the strategy of identifying the item(s) you looked at and then showing you ads for those items as you continue to explore other sites online. Many large companies, especially online retailers, now incorporate re-targeting as a primary marketing channel.

Until recently this type of advertising was not accessible to local business. Part of that was the cost of producing and distributing advertisements. More important was the fact that the technology had not yet been developed to the point where a specific market niche and local business market area could be pinpointed with accuracy.

That has all changed! A local spa can now offer services on the Home and Garden channel. Want to see your roofing business on the ESPN website...no problem. Do many of your customers frequent weather.com? Why not invite them to your business by publishing your ads on weather.com?

There are several categories of banner advertising available to your business, but before I describe them I want to take just a minute and talk about the technology that makes all of this possible. The analogy that I'll use is the stock market and the New York Stock Exchange.

If you own a business and want to "go public" you can't just print off a bunch of stock certificates, run an ad in USA Today, and start selling shares. (Well, you probably could, but it wouldn't take long for an attorney from the SEC to contact you.) To take your company public requires that you prepare an Initial Public Offering document and have brokers who are willing to represent your company to their customers and "market" your business to prospective investors. Then your shares have to be accepted for trade by an "exchange." The one most of us are familiar with is the New York Stock Exchange, but there are other exchanges that process trades with smaller capitalization stocks.

When someone wants to buy your stock they contact a broker who consults the exchange to see what the current market price of your stock is, and if there are any available shares to purchase. If you own the stock and want to sell some shares you do the same thing, contact a broker who will make your shares available to the exchange. The price of the stock fluctuates based on supply and demand.

All those ads from Amazon and the multitude of companies who purchase ad space online get to your computer screen or mobile phone in much the same way. There are several primary "ad exchanges" that function just like the stock exchanges. Companies who want to "monetize" their websites offer to sell ad space on the site. They join one or more of the exchanges and make their "ad space inventory" available. Companies who want to advertise create a set of banner ads and submit them to the ad exchanges for approval. Once approved, your ads go into the ad inventory and are placed on websites in a competitive bidding process that is almost like an auction.

Here's an example. You own a heating and air conditioning company in Oklahoma City, but you also serve several communities in the OKC metro area. You want to begin buying online ad inventory in one category, re-targeting. You contact an agency that is approved to sell to the ad exchanges who designs several sets of ads for you and submits them to the exchanges. A day or so later your ads are approved. Now here's where the magic starts.

Your agency has done a proper analysis of the competition in your market area and identified the specific zip codes that you want to have ads displayed in (this is a 'geographic' campaign). They have also created a "re-targeting pixel" and added it to your website. This is a snippet of computer code, html code to be exact, that is placed just before the closing <Head>/ tag in the header of your websites home page. Everyone who visits your website will then be "pixeled" with this code.

As the visitor leaves your website and goes to another, the ad exchanges will determine if they are within the geographical area that you've set for your campaigns. Then they look at the website your visitor is now on to see if it is a site that accepts ads. If it is, then they look at the available ad size configurations available on that site. The next step is to analyze all of the companies that are competing for that ad space regardless of type of campaign. They then evaluate the dollar amount of the "bid" for ad space made by each of these companies and determine a winner. That company's ad is then displayed in front of the visitor. As the visitor to your site continues to search around the web this process is repeated for every website they visit.

What is amazing about this process is that everything I just described happens in roughly 40 milli-seconds—less than the time it takes to load the website onto the visitors screen! One of the reasons this marketing channel was only available to larger companies was the limitation on available bandwidth and Internet speed. That is no longer the case, and as with any "open market" now that there is an increased supply of ad inventory more participating companies are needed to buy it up.

The opportunity for a small business today is the reality that the majority of business owners don't yet know about this, and just a small percentage of advertising and marketing agencies have the technology platforms to offer it. That heating contractor in Oklahoma City I used as an example earlier can grab a significant market share just by being an early adopter of this technology!

Here's a couple of take-aways from what I've said so far about banner advertising:

1. This is a new opportunity. I like to think of it as Google in 2006, a wide-open playing field where the first businesses to take advantage of the technology will prosper.
2. The exchanges are not available to a business owner to work with directly. (The lone exception is the Google

Ad Exchange which can be accessed much like their Adwords platform that I described earlier.) However, as ubiquitous as Google is in the search world, their ad platform is a small player. You must have an agency that is registered with at least one of the exchanges to 'represent' you and get your ads considered. You want an agency that participates in as many agencies as possible, so you have more opportunities for ad placement.

3. Developing the "creatives," that is, the display ads, isn't as easy as having your graphics person put an ad together. First, the available ad inventory on all websites must conform to one of 16 different sizes. Many sites will accept ads of different sizes on the same page. The placement on the page factors into the cost of the ad as well. Prime exposure near the top of the page is more expensive than a smaller ad on the sidebar, for example. When you submit a set of ads for approval that set must include all 16 of the standard sizes.

4. To further complicate things, all ads must feature either the advertising companies logo or phone number. Images must be "compliant" with the ad exchange guidelines (which means generic images that are not likely to offend anyone). Images must be 150 kb or smaller so that they load quickly.

5. A recent update, again based on the increased speed of the internet, are animated ads and video ads. Animated ads are not like cartoons, but ads with one component of the ad that changes as it is displayed. A call to action button that switches between yellow and brown and then back to yellow for example. Video ads

can only be displayed on limited number of sites at this time, which means they are more expensive to include in a campaign.

Categories of Banner Advertising

The most obvious, re-targeting, I've already described. Someone visits your website, a pixel is "dropped" onto their device, and your ads are shown to them for a period of time (set by you and your agency).

The other primary category of Banner advertising is Cold Market ad placement. These campaigns are designed to attract the attention of someone who has not yet been to your website and invite them to visit. Here your agency creates sets of ads and submits them to the exchanges. Once approved they are placed based on your specifications for the campaign. These can be:

1. Geographic. Usually designated by zip code, your ads will only be shown to people who live within the specific zip codes. Almost any business or professional practice can benefit from geographic targeting of the area around their business location, or a specific neighborhood they'd like to expand into. We have found this to be especially effective for home improvement contractors who target neighborhoods.
2. Demographic. If you want to make your business known to people who are interested in gardening, that can be done. Or homeowners with children still at home who have a family income over $75,000…easy. What about people who like classic cars? No problem. I hope you're seeing that if you have carefully identified one or more ideal customers for your product or service

it is very likely that a highly focused campaign that only targets those people can be developed. Of course you can combine geographic criteria with demographic.
3. Specific sites. What if you just want your ads displayed on a few specific websites? Like the local network affiliates, ESPN, Zillow, etc. A campaign just offering your ads to those sites can be designed.
4. Hyper-local campaigns. This is where you identify a specific address and small area around it for your ads to be presented. For example, you sell products to dentists. There is a dental convention coming up next month in St. Louis at the convention center. We would design banners inviting convention attendees to your booth or presentation, or just exposing your products if you don't have a booth. We take the address of the convention center and say a radius around it of 1500 feet (to get the convention hotels that the dentists are likely to be staying at.) Your ads start running the day before the convention through one day after it is over. This highly targeted style of campaign will only display on mobile devices, but that's OK because your potential customers are moving around the convention center and using their phones to stay in touch.
5. There is one more option that is available after several months of campaigns. We use software to manage banner ad campaigns that track every website where a prospect clicked on the ad. Over time we find the top dozen or so sites that seem to have the most potential customers for our client. We then create new campaigns and target just those sites.

Sounds Complicated...Are Banner Ads Expensive ?

I've saved the best for last. If you have any experience with PPC or Facebook advertising you know how quickly you can go through money. Depending on the niche your business is in, an ad budget of $3000 may not be enough to stay competitive.

Banner advertising is priced differently. Rather than a cost per click, you pay a fee for each 1000 impressions. Since this is still a fairly new marketplace, I tell our customers to plan on about $25 ad spend per thousand impressions. There are exceptions of course. If animated ads are included in your campaigns the cost will be more. Video ads, because of supply and demand, are currently running $100 per thousand impressions. We have seen these budget amounts increase over the last twelve months as more and more companies come into the market, so expect to see that trend continue.

Fortunately, there are specific controls you can implement to "throttle" the ad spend. I've already discussed limiting the geographical reach of your ads. You can also specify how many times in a day one person sees your ad, and/or the times during the day that your ad is shown.

Another consideration that is important to factor into your thinking is the reality of "banner blindness." This describes the fact that after someone sees your ad a couple of times they don't see it again. Or at least they won't focus on it. That is why it is important that your agency develop multiple sets of ads and rotate them frequently.

Let me elaborate on this point. How many ad sets do you need? How frequently should they be changed? The more important question is, "how long does the typical prospect take to make a decision about what you sell?" If it is a relatively short time then you don't need more than a couple of ad sets. Longer, you'll need more.

Here's how our agency answers that question. If your buyer typically spends 14 days or less making a decision we prepare five distinct sets of ads. At least one of these will feature one of your five-star reviews, another with an offer of some kind, and the remaining three are more "branding" ads designed to keep your company name in front of the prospect. This means we rotate a new ad set into place every two days for the first six days, give the remaining two sets three days "online," and then run the first set again for the last two days.

Between 14- and 30-day decision making time we create ten sets of ads, just double the number of each ad type. These we run for three days each. Some clients have prospects who take longer to make a decision, a plastic surgeon client comes to mind. We run their ten ad sets for the thirty days, during which time we're monitoring the traffic that each ad set generates. At the end of the month we replace the lowest five sets with new ones and continue until the prospect makes a decision.

What should a local business expect to budget for a complete campaign? By complete campaign I mean analysis of your business niche and geographical location, development of multiple ad sets, design of the campaign specifics and daily monitoring of results, A/B split testing of ads, and monthly reporting to you. The starting point is going to be $750 for a retargeting campaign including the ad spend. For more diversified campaigns that include retargeting as well as other cold market campaigns the monthly cost will range up to $2000, again including the ad spend. Of course these estimates will change as the market evolves.

What Results Should You Expect from Banner Advertising?

Our agency started with banner advertising in 2014. At that time it was called RTB (Real Time Bidding) and we could only offer it to regional clients who served a larger geographical footprint because it wasn't possible to narrow it down. There were fewer websites that accepted advertising, so the costs were significantly higher. Our campaigns at that time started at $4500 for just retargeting.

What a better marketplace we have today! I have often shared with groups that I'm speaking with that "retargeting is the only marketing strategy that makes all of your other marketing more effective!" It should be obvious that I'm bullish on retargeting and banner advertising as a strategy for just about any business or professional practice.

That being said, how can a business owner measure the value, the ROI, of banner campaign advertising? Here are some considerations:

1. Increased brand exposure
2. More clicks, because you have many more ads in more places
3. Direct hits onto your domain
4. Increased landing page effectiveness (with more hits)
5. Branded search increases (searches that include all/part of company name)
6. Domain.com searches (powerful for SEO)

7. Overall increase in calls, visits, emails, chats.

All of which means: more sales!

Many marketing channels are great for building your brand (radio, TV, your website, billboards, citation and directory sites, your online reputation, etc). Others are good for creating sales (PPC, direct mail, email blasts, print ads, etc). Only retargeting and banner advertising do both. My encouragement to you as a business owner is that you prioritize learning more about this marketing channel and consider adding it to your business growth strategy.

"There are no traffic jams along the extra mile"

--Roger Staubach

Social Media—Marketing Tool or Time Suck?

In the last year we have experienced a tremendous increase in the number of conversations and inquiries about social media. Most business owners know that they need to have a presence on social media but are not sure where to start. Those that have tried are quickly overwhelmed with the amount of work involved in curating and creating content, publishing on multiple platforms, following up with responses—it becomes a job in itself.

A frequent, and usually unsuccessful, solution is to have a young member of your team become the "social media person" for the company. "After all," you may be thinking, "they seem to be on Facebook all the time!"

I say usually unsuccessful because the messaging that is frequently distributed may not be what you as the owner really want to be said about your company. Then there is the problem with employee turnover. What happens when your social media person leaves the company, or just stops showing up? Does anyone else know how to get into the accounts and change the passwords? We've witnessed several instances where the employee managing Facebook posts becomes disgruntled over something and sends out a flurry of posts detrimental to the company.

If you are one of those business owners that is feeling overwhelmed by social media and not sure where to start, I'm going to offer some easy to implement solutions in this chapter. For those who feel that it takes a big budget for advertising and branding on social media I have hope as well. It doesn't, but you need a solid plan in place before you start to make sure you control costs.

Let me start with some reasons why every business needs to consider adding social media to their marketing plan. The statistics are compelling:

- 71% of consumers who have had a good social media service experience with a brand are likely to recommend it to others. (Source: Ambassador)
- Visual content is more than 40x more likely to get shared on social media than any other type of content. (Source: HubSpot)
- 90.4% of Millennials use social media daily. 77.5% Gen X. 48.2% Baby Boomers. (Source: Emarketer 2019)

For most businesses it is no longer an option to have at least a basic presence on social media. Which leads to the next obvious question, "how many social media platforms do I need to be active on?" For the answer to this question I will say again the point I emphasized in the first chapter of this book: who is your ideal customer? What social media platforms are they visiting on a regular basis? Those are the platforms you need to be on!

Let me be more specific and address the major social media platforms. I know there are more than these, but from a business owners perspective these are the primary places to evaluate:

Facebook: every business and professional practice needs a Facebook business page.

LinkedIn: I feel every business owner should have a basic LinkedIn profile. Keep in mind your profile is not your resume! Rather, it is a place for you to share the value proposition(s) for your business and why other business owners should consider connecting with you.

Instagram: do you have a high percentage of Millennials as customers? You need to be here.

Twitter: for most business owners this is not necessary. If you're in the hospitality arena you can take advantage of the immediacy of posting to your Twitter followers, but most industries will not need this platform. Even so, there are two reasons to consider using Twitter. First is that when you post you can create backlinks to your website, a landing page, or offer that you are promoting. This can augment your efforts to get your sites found online. Second, Twitter is an easy place to use @links to keep up with things happening in your industry.

YouTube: I have a whole chapter later in the book on the importance and value of video. If you have any video for you business, or hope to have in the future, then creating a YouTube channel is important.

Reddit: This is an interesting option. When you post content on Reddit it is voted on by other users. Popular content stays visible, less popular gets pushed down in the results. The reason a business should consider posting to Reddit is what are called "subreddits." These are boards dedicated to specific topics. An example: if you have a veterinary practice you could create real value by participating in a board on pet care.

Tumblr: 39% of visitors are under the age of 25, another 26% between 25 and 35 years old. A content ban at the end of 2018 significantly impeded the growth of Tumblr, and usage lags far behind the other platforms I've listed. Unless you specifically target a younger demographic like "young parents" you don't need to be here.

Google Business Page: While not technically a "social media" site, your GMB page accepts posts, images, and video. Google has placed a lot of emphasis on using this page, so if you're going to have a social media program it makes sense to include GMB.

Another way to think about social media and the specific sites to consider working with is the fact that each one becomes a digital storefront for your business. The same customers than walk into your physical location are going to find value in your social media "store."

Social Media is a "Top of Mind" Strategy

I want to transition now from talking about the different social media platforms to how you can best use them as part of your marketing. Perhaps the most important fact to keep in mind when it comes to social media marketing is that your posts are a "top of mind" strategy. What does that mean? Simply this: your posts disappear quickly. You must post frequently and across platforms to keep your name and brand in front of potential customers.

This is an essential difference between social media and other marketing channels. Your website is easy to find every day.

Video content can be searched and watched today, next week, or next year. But social media posts are like radio ads—they are gone quickly. That doesn't mean that someone can't scroll and find an old post, but with the volume of content being uploaded to these platforms hourly it is less likely that someone will do this.

This brings up the obvious question: how often do I need to post? Here's the general policy we follow for our clients:

> Twitter: 4x daily
> Facebook: 2x daily
> LinkedIn: 1x daily
> Instagram: 3x daily
> GMB: 1x daily

The reason we do this is because a typical post will only be seen by 12% of your followers. Making multiple posts of the same content will increase the likelihood that it is being engaged with by your ideal customers. A second reason is that social networks promote consistency.

As a business owner you are not considering a social media strategy just to be cool, your efforts need to have a realistic chance of generating new business. How do you do that? According to broadbandsearch.net, who interviewed several thousand users of social media across all age ranges and learned some interesting things:

> 48% of people said that "being responsive" will encourage them to buy
> 46% said offering promotions
> 42% said providing educational content
> 27% said providing "behind the scenes" content

26% said being funny

Another way to interpret this study is simply that your social media content needs to be engaging and focused on bringing value to the viewer. How do you do that?

I'm going to share with you in some detail the process we follow here at Alchemy for curating/creating content for our clients. In doing so I encourage you to take this process and implement it for your own business. If you have questions, remember that I offer a free one-hour consult for anyone who reads this book. You'll find my contact information after the last chapter.

We use an acronym, "RECIPE"* as a guideline for creating and publishing content. Here's what that means:

<u>Recreational</u> content is the more humorous component in your strategy. This might include jokes relevant to your business niche, recognition of holidays, funny cartoons or graphics (again related to your business niche) or an interesting historical note for something that happened on this day.

<u>Educational</u> content could be tips and tricks you offer that are connected to what you do, facts or interesting trivia, case studies, trends and research that might be of interest to a broad spectrum of your readers. Your goal is for people to stop and think, "wow, I didn't know that."

<u>Conversational</u> content is a place to ask for advice from your followers or ask them questions. You can post surveys or polls, This vs That content, really anything that gets people talking with each other and engaging with the content, and

subconsciously with your brand.

Inspirational posts are interesting quotes from famous and not so famous people, client success stories, before/after images or stories, and inspiring images that evoke the basic humanity that we all share.

Do you notice anything about these first four categories of posts? I haven't suggested you say anything about your company; no promotions or offers or chest beating. Why? The point is to engage your audience with you in a way that is not 'salesy.' Remember, people love to buy but hate to be sold.

Promotional. OK, now we start to get more specific about your company. With promotional content you can feature your 5-star reviews, invite people to attend a live demonstration or webinar, make a specific offer or give a discount. This is where you can begin to take the good will you've been creating with the other categories of posts and invite your readers to become customers.

Entrepreneurial posts continue to focus more on your business. Here you can share your mission, vision, and values. Posts featuring an employee or partner are effective at demonstrating the humanness of your business. Sharing something about your personal life, jogging with your dog for example, will help people relate to you as the owner of your business.

We have found this formula to be an antidote to the consistent shrill promotions that many companies use social media for. At the same time, it is important to invite prospects to engage and become customers, so just posting puppy videos isn't enough either!

If you decide to utilize the RECIPE formula let me also suggest the frequency you should consider for each type of post. For most businesses posting during the business week is adequate, some choose to also publish on Saturday. Whether you spread your posts across five or six days, I would do so like this:

> Recreational: 6 posts/week
> Educational: 5 posts/week
> Conversational: 4 posts/week
> Inspirational: 3 posts/week
> Promotional: 2 posts/week
> Entrepreneurial: 1 post/week

You may be looking at this schedule and wondering if there are enough calls to buy. My answer is yes, over time this formula will generate customers. Social media posting is a process of engagement, of brand development and acceptance over time...it is not a used car lot.

One more insight about social media I'd like to share. At the top of the page for most of your sites is a header area. If you are like 99% of your competitors, you put some information and maybe a photo here when you initially built the site and haven't thought about it since.

That's a mistake. If the point of your social media posting, and the time/cost you are investing, is to create a relationship with prospects and turn them into customers why are you not using this giant "billboard" at the top of your sites as a marketing tool? You want people continue to come back to your site, show them something different on a regular basis.

A few weeks before the 4th of July create a patriotic banner. For Halloween or Thanksgiving or any other holiday you can easily do the same. Having an end of summer promotion? Create a header that tells people about it. Many veterinarians participate in the February canine teeth cleaning promotion. If your practice is doing this announce it starting in the middle of January and encourage people to make appointments.

I'm sure you see my point. This is valuable marketing space that has a lot of eyes on it. Take advantage of that by rotating your images and content throughout the year. We do this as a part of our Social Media programs for our clients, so here again if you have questions let me know.

I started this chapter by offering hope to business owners that are feeling overwhelmed by social media. If you design a program for curating and creating content along the lines of the RECIPE formula, and implementing a consistent posting program, I am confident that in a very short time you will begin to see the benefits from this effort.

*The "RECIPE" formula was originally created by Real Strategic, an international marketing agency based in Florida.

Core 5® Marketing

"If you want to know what John Smith buys, you have to see the world through John Smith's eyes."

--Jack Driscoll

Video Marketing--Putting the World's #2 Search Engine to Work for You

While not one of the Core 5® marketing categories that I describe in this book, I'm including a chapter on video because it is so important. Video is also closely connected to each of the other Core 5® channels. For example, we routinely produce Reputation Marketing videos using one of the 5-star reviews our clients have received. Including 30 second videos in your Facebook posts or on your Google Business page will increase engagement with your social media. We incorporate video into many of our traffic campaigns. Video is a powerful tool for helping your primary website get found online. Video has become such in integral component in a complete marketing plan that I want to give you some insights in how to use it.

Not too many years ago, if you thought about "video marketing" your only option was to produce and broadcast television commercials. While expensive, for many roofing companies it was the best way to get prospects calling. As local cable advertising rates and video production costs have dropped, this can still be a powerful business growth strategy for you company.

Here's some good news: you don't have to hire an ad agency and expensive camera crews to produce top quality marketing videos anymore. In fact, with a smart phone and just a little creativity you can create dynamic marketing pieces that will inform, teach, engage, and amuse people. Nor do you need to buy a package of airtime from your local cable provider. Now you can "broadcast" your videos on YouTube, Vimeo, Daily Motion, Hulu, and at least a dozen more video websites.

In this chapter I want to demonstrate the importance and simplicity of video marketing for your business. Here's how I'm going to do that:

- Some startling facts showing why you need video marketing
- Types of videos to shoot
- How to get started producing quality videos for your business
- How to Set up a YouTube channel
- Strategies for marketing your videos

Why You Need Video Marketing

If you have any doubts about video as a marketing tool for your company, here are some facts compiled in early 2017, along with the sources of the data:

- YouTube has 2 billion visitors each month. (Huff Post)
- Just under 5 billion videos are watched on YouTube each day (Videoniche)
- 52% of consumers say that watching a video makes them more confident in online purchases (Inovodo)
- 55% of marketers who use video in their email campaigns reported an increase in click through rate (eMarketer)

- 9% of US Small businesses use YouTube (FortuneLords)
- 82% of marketers plan to add video to their sites, making it a higher priority than Facebook, Twitter, and blog integration (Social Media Examiner)
- Videos on landing pages increased conversions by 86% (WebDAM)

So the question is no longer, "do I need any videos to market my business?" The question should be, "how can I incorporate video into my company marketing quickly and easily?"

Video? What Do I Do That Should Be on A Video?

You may be surprised to learn that most of what you do in your business is worth shooting a short video about. Remember that many times when people are searching for the product or service that you offer they don't know enough about your business to even know what to ask. What they want to do is find someone they feel they can trust to do a good job at a fair price. The purpose of your video marketing is to let them get to know you, your team, and the quality of work you do.

Video is far more compelling than anything written you can put on your website to facilitate this "know-like-trust" process.

Here are some ideas for types of videos you might consider:

1. Testimonials. Perhaps the most powerful marketing you can do is a short video with a customer. These are quite simple to shoot and require almost no preparation. "After the job is finished" interviews with the customer are particularly effective for contractors and home improvement companies. Here are some tips for this type of video:

- An ideal length is 30 to 45 seconds. This gives you enough time to ask no more than two questions and let the homeowner respond.
- If outdoors, you'll be shooting using the natural light available that day. Make sure not to shoot in such a way that the sun is behind the people or their faces will be obscured. If indoors it is best to place the homeowner near a window and get as much natural light as possible. Remember, florescent lights show as a nasty yellow color on video. Incandescent bulbs are more forgiving but can be a little blue. As much natural light as possible is best.
- If you're shooting outdoors, the job you've done should be in the background. The new roof, garage door, sunroom, pool, whatever the nature of the service was should be featured in the video.
- There are two ways to do these videos, and creating a library that is a mixture of both is best. One is to have the crew manager standing with the people, look to the camera and introduce them, ask one or two questions, say thank you, and it's done. It is a very quick conversation where they are looking at each other, not into the camera once the introduction is made. In this scene another crew member will shoot the video.
- The second method is to have the homeowner(s) only in the shot, let them introduce themselves, and then mention two things they especially appreciated about your company, the crew, and the job. You will prompt them with the subjects before they start, but there is

not someone asking them questions, it is their "candid" impressions. In this case they will be looking into the camera.

The questions and subjects we want people to address are the "hot buttons" that are in the minds of prospective customers who will be watching these. For example:

- Protecting plants, windows, patio, etc when doing the work in the landscape or outside of the home
- Getting good value for the money spent, a quality job with quality materials
- Are the crews professional looking and talking, or are they derelicts off the street covered in ink and swearing at each other all day (if I'm a husband and my wife stays at home, am I comfortable with her being there alone with these guys?)

2. Owner/Personality. This type of video features the owner of the business, or a sales manager if he/she is more comfortable in front of the camera. No matter who you decide to use, it is important that the majority of your videos feature that person. They become the "face" of your company to the community. Again, some tips:

- These can be a little longer, depending on the subject matter. 60 to 120 seconds is a good length, unless you are demonstrating something that take longer and is interesting to the potential viewer.
- Focus on subjects that will have meaning to someone looking for what you sell. Do not shoot platitude filled "commercials" about how you are the 'best in town.' It's fine to ask for their business but give them a

compelling reason to take the next step in the sales process with you.
- Feature other members of the team, especially as you develop a good size library of videos. For example, Mary in accounting is having her 20th anniversary with the company this month. Do a short video introducing Mary and acknowledging her long service. This type of video will show people a more human side of your business.
- Some of these should be shot "in the field," others "in the studio." Proper planning in advance will result in a library of videos that are meaningful to a prospect and generate interest in your company.

3. Demonstrations. This genre of video is particularly valuable if you are in a business where you can demonstrate what you do or show specific tools/equipment you use in your business. These videos are powerful generators of trust and do a great job of establishing you as an expert who is willing to share their knowledge.

As an example, we worked with a dentist who specialized in designing custom mouth pieces worn by people who were dealing with sleep apnea. He had a very particular type of MRI machine that did a full head scan. At that time there were only two in the state, his and one at the university hospital. We shot a 2-minute video with the doctor, in his white coat, introducing the equipment and then demonstrating how it worked with a "patient" (it was yours truly) sitting in the seat. It was a great way to set his practice apart from every competitor.

If you are a contractor or any business that works in situations where safety equipment is required, make certain that everyone on your team that is included in the videos is wearing all of the safety equipment that is required or necessary. You would not want to have an accident at some time in the future and have your own marketing videos used as an example of how you ignore safety protocols!

If you think about it for just a minute, I'm sure you can come up with several ideas for this type of video. Now I'll share with you how to convert these ideas into top quality videos

How to Get Started Producing Quality Videos for Your Business

When I talk with clients about video they immediately assume they'll need a lot of expensive equipment or have to hire a specialist to produce them. Not the case anymore. To begin producing quality videos that will show your company in a positive light you only need two things: some basic equipment and a video plan.

When I say basic equipment I would bet that you already have the most important piece, the camera. That's right, if you have a relatively recent smart phone, either an iPhone or an Android, you already have a camera that will give you quality raw video footage. There are those who say that one format is better than another. Honestly, I can't tell the difference between a finished video that was shot on an iPhone from one that was taken with an Android. So whichever one you own, use it.

As you begin to produce more video content, you may want to add some additional equipment. If you are going to create video in a room in your office, you will want a "green screen" background. Without going into a lot of videographer jargon, this is a solid color that you stand in front of when shooting the video. This neutral color will help your viewer focus on the subject of the video, you or the props you are demonstrating. Using very simple video production software (you probably already have this) it is an easy matter to superimpose your video over another background by replacing the "green screen" digitally.

You can search online for a photographers supply company and buy a fabric green screen and the rack system to support it, but that's not necessary. You can buy sheets of material from a fabric store and create your own. Even simpler is to head over to the hardware store and buy a gallon of dinosaur green paint in the kids section and paint one wall. (Make sure it is a smooth wall, not textured, or you will not be able to light it easily.)

A tripod to hold your phone/camera steady when shooting is important. Since your phone is lightweight, you don't need to invest in a heavy professional style tripod. Most phones have an adaptor that they fit in that will mount into the tripod's quick release. Or there are holders that you phone will slip into that can be attached to the tripod. You may have to go online to find this.

For indoor shooting having control of the light is important. You want to eliminate shadows cast by the subject against the background. Here again you can go to a photographers supply company and buy studio lights. Alien Bees is a company that manufactures a very inexpensive but accurate studio lighting, we use them in our indoor studio. But you don't need to go to that level. I've seen great video produced using the halogen shop lights you can get at Home Depot or Lowes for less than $50. You'll have to experiment with distance from the subject since these do not have the light intensity adjustments of regular photographers studio lights.

Most important is sound quality. Your viewers will overlook average video quality, or a little camera shake, but if they have to struggle to hear what is being said they will click away in seconds. Invest some money in a good quality wireless microphone. You can expect to pay around $125 for a system that will synch into your phone/camera. Do not try to skip this expense. Whether you do most of your videos indoors or outside, good audio quality is critical.

A video editing software program will be necessary for any "studio" style videos you produce. Fortunately, you probably already have a good basic program. If you use a Windows based computer then Windows Movie Maker is already loaded and ready to use. For Mac users, iMovie is your included tool. Both are pretty intuitive and have good help tools.

Another option are programs produced by TechSmith. They have a free program you can download, Jing, that will do screen capture videos of up to five minutes. An alternative that does the same thing is Loom. For a more versatile, and complicated, solution consider a program like Camtasia (techsmith.com). This is a complete video editing platform that gives you total control over the finished product. You can upload video files from your phone for editing or create longer screen captures. We also use this program in our office to produce video webinars. The retail cost for Camtasia is about $250.

That's it. With those equipment basics you are ready to be the Steven Spielberg for your company. To produce quality videos that accurately represent the good name of your company you need more than just equipment. You'll also need a plan to create engaging videos that will hold the interest of your prospects. Here are some tips for how to do that:

1. Quality videos don't happen by accident. They're created with pre-production planning. The following are a must:

- Shot list. Take a legal pad and write down the different shots you want to include in your video. It may only be one or two for a short video but plan them
- Story board. Make a simple sketch of any complex shots or transitions between shots. This is especially important if you're shooting "on location."
- Prop list per scene. A professional looking finished product will be the result if you have everything you're going to need ready before starting the camera.
- B-roll. This is additional footage that will make your story come to life when it comes time to edit. Some examples might include showing your crew getting ready at the start of the job, you driving to a job site and talking to the camera held by one of your people in the passenger seat, walking around your building with equipment and activity in the background as you answer common questions. Touring your treatment rooms and highlighting some of the equipment you use with patients.

2. **Be clear and give a reason to stick around.** Make sure viewers know in the first five to 10 seconds exactly why they should keep watching. Tell them and show the benefits they'll get from watching your video. Even for a short, 45 to 90 second video, have an attention getting headline as you begin. People have very short attention spans when sitting in front of their computers.

3. **Be Energetic.** People who demonstrate passion and energy on camera are more likely to hold a viewer's attention than being monotone and dull. Just watch any stand-up comedian and see how his or her energy affects an audience.

Try speaking a bit louder than normal and be a little more animated with your body language. Don't mumble. Look at the camera when appropriate, at the work you are demonstrating, and then back at the camera.

All this might feel strange in front of the camera but can create a more engaging video. It may take a little practice but is worth the time.

4. **Postproduction.** Once you have your video footage shot, what do you do with it? In some cases, like "on the job" testimonials from customers, they are ready to go without any postproduction work. Other times you will want to load the .mp4 file into your editing software and adjust as needed.

If you decide to make video an important part of your company marketing, then you'll want to have a channel trailer and outro created. A channel trailer is a short, 10 seconds or less, clip that "brands" your company and your channel. An outro is another clip that typically shows your company name, phone number, and website address. This clip should be seven to ten seconds in length so people can see how to contact you if they want to. Every video you produce should have the intro and outro added as a part of your postproduction work.

If you've never used a website called fiverr (www.fiverr.com) I recommend it. This is a job site with literally thousands of workers around the world who are offering their services to do work on a per job basis. After you log into the site look in the "video and animation" category to find someone to create your channel trailer.

Once you have your videos created and produced, then next step is to upload them to your channel on the key video sites on the internet.

Creating Your YouTube Channel

Producing a library of marketing videos is the first step, now you need a place for prospects to find and watch them. Enter YouTube, Vimeo, Daily Motion, Hulu, and a host of other websites that are designed to display video. The best way to combine making your videos available along with enhancing your company brand is to create a channel on these sites. I'm going to talk about YouTube, but the process is similar with the other sites.

How many sites do you need? Really, just one: YouTube. It is the second largest search engine in the world, based on number of searches conducted. The last statistics I read indicated that YouTube controlled almost 85% of the online video marketplace. The value in also creating a channel and posting your videos to one or two other sites is that the search engine spiders do crawl them, and there is page rank value in being found on multiple sites. We use an automated video posting software program for our clients, but still only upload videos to three of the sites (YouTube, Vimeo, Daily Motion.)

Creating a YouTube channel is an easy process you should be able to complete is less than a half hour. The best advice I can suggest is to do a Google search for, "how to create a YouTube channel for my business." Then look at the publishing date of all the links that come up to find the most recent. I say this because the process changes often, especially as Google continues to integrate their various tools and programs. (If you didn't know, Google owns YouTube.) Ironically, you should be able to find a YouTube video showing you how to create a channel on YouTube.

Strategies for Marketing Your Videos

Once you've created your Video Channel, here are some best practices for using it as a marketing tool.

1. How should I organize my video content?
Instead of presenting your videos in a single long list, group them into playlists by topic or theme. Some topics might include: Customer Testimonials, "Demonstrations," Our Company, etc. With a little navigation, viewers can more easily find videos that interest them.

2. How often should I post videos?
Upload new videos as often as your schedule and budget allow, especially as you are getting started. Once you have a library of a dozen or more in your channel, you might create

a publishing schedule and then announce on your website and through social media every time you publish a new video.

3. How do I customize my channel background?

When designing your YouTube channel try to mirror your company's existing online look, including the color schemes and logos on your website. You can choose a background color for your channel and then upload your background image. This congruence will help establish your brand in the local market.

4. Should I upload commercials about my products and services?

People come to YouTube to be entertained, educated and informed, but not to watch commercials. The idea is to put helpful, informative videos on YouTube that enhance your company's image without being overly promotional. It is good to have a call to action, that is one of the reasons to add an outro slide to every video. That slide should have your company name, address, phone number, and website address. Leave the outro slide in view for the last five to ten seconds of your video.

There is a distinct difference between a commercial about your product and a "how to use" video that helps people quickly implement your product or learn more about what it might do for them. This style of video should be informative only. You can finish with a sentence that is, "if you have questions you can find us online or call 555-555-1212." Then finish the video with your outro slide.

5. How should I describe and tag my videos?

When you upload an mp4 file to YouTube their software will format it to YouTube standards and create a unique identifier, like a URL, for that video. Once the video is available on YouTube you want to optimize by adding a title, description, and tags. The title should be the subject of the video, for example: Dog Grooming. I also like to add the company name and phone number if they both will fit into the space allowed. A title might look like this: Dog Grooming with Toni, 555-555-1212.

The video description is a place to let the potential viewer know more about what the video is about, as well as list your company contact information. Using appropriate keywords for your business is important, but generally no more than three of your keywords in each description. At the time I'm writing this you are allowed up to 600 characters in the description box. I always try to fill the box with relevant information.

YouTube has 'spiders' that crawl all video content just like the search engines have spiders that crawl all the pages of a website. There are different opinions as to how much of the description box these spiders crawl. Some believe it is only the first two sentences, others say the entire area. When I'm writing video descriptions I split the difference. That is, I make sure the first two sentences are carefully worded and include my most important keywords for that video. Then I write the rest of the sentences to get as close as possible to the 600-character limit. I always like to include the website address and telephone number somewhere near the bottom of the description.

The "Tags" area under the description box is where you can put a series of keywords. I like to include a location with some of these, like Veterinarian Albuquerque. You also want to include keywords that are relevant to the subject of the video. For example, if you're posting an on-the-job video showing chimney repair, add keyword tags like "chimney," "chimney repair," "flashing" "chimney cap" and "roof repair." That way searchers can easily find it via search engines and YouTube search.

When optimizing your video you'll also see a tab for "Advanced." Most people do not complete this area, but YouTube values the information and uses it in search placement, so I always complete it. Here is how I enter information on this page.

> Comments: I check this to allow comments, and allow all except potentially inappropriate comments, with the newest first.
>
> Users can view ratings: I check this allowing future viewers to see the ratings.
>
> License and Rights: Standard YouTube license. This protects your content from others using some or all in their own videos.
>
> Caption Certification: I always select the first option. If your video has been used on television you will choose another.
>
> Distribution Options: I check both.

Age restrictions: I do not check this, we do not produce any video where someone under 18 shouldn't see it.

Category: I typically use Education or People and Blogs.

Video Location: this is very important! Enter your office address so that your videos will be 'geo-tagged' by YouTube.

Video Language: English (assuming it is in English)

Community Contributions: Do not check this box.

Recording Date: Enter the date the video was made, or the upload date.

Video Statistics: I do not check this box.

Content Declaration: I do not use paid placements in my videos, so I do not check this box.

This may seem like extra work that doesn't really impact the potential customer who is watching the video, but it may help get your video placed higher in the search results. A completely optimized video will also be offered more frequently by YouTube than one that is not properly optimized.

6. Should I allow comments on my videos?

Allowing people to comment on your videos should encourage them to share their experiences with your brand and show that you're open to feedback. You can automatically display comments, display them only after you've approved them or keep them hidden. If you enable comments, you still have the option to delete any that are inappropriate or spammy.

Just like Facebook and other social media sites, the comments section is where you directly interact with and engage your community. If you allow comments realize that it's important to respond in the most helpful and authentic way possible, which means someone in your company is going to have to monitor your channel(s) regularly.

7. How should I promote my channel?

Every time you upload a new video, share a direct link to it across all your business's social media networks. You can embed your YouTube videos and playlists in your business's website or blog.

You can also try to build an audience for your videos with Google Adwords for video, which lets you create and manage video promotions on YouTube and elsewhere online. Google Adwords campaigns are cost-per-view (CPV). To set a CPV bid, you enter the highest price you want to pay. For example, if you think it's worth 25 cents for someone to watch your video, set that amount as your maximum CPV. Then you pay only when people watch your video.

8. How can I measure my channel's success?

YouTube offers a free, self-service viewership analytics and reporting tool called YouTube Analytics. It tells you how many people watch your videos, how often, and how they discovered your videos.

YouTube Analytics also shows you how many subscribers you have, as well as how many likes, dislikes, comments and shares each video has received. Tracking which videos are most popular, along with the precise moment people stop watching them, can help you learn which types of content resonate with your viewers.

One Final Tip:

Consistently creating quality video content is a powerful marketing tool that can augment your other marketing channels. Something as a business owner you might consider is finding a part time studying film or communications at the local Junior College. They would love the "real world" experience, and this will help you ensure that the quality of your video content is good. What you don't want to do is get excited about the potential of video, produce a couple, then get busy and not do anything for six months. As is true in other marketing channels, consistency of publishing is critical.

Core 5® Marketing

"If you change your language, you'll change your business."

--David Sprague

Getting Found Online, Solving the Search Engine Puzzle

If you've been in business more than a couple of weeks, you have undoubtedly answered the phone only to find it was "Julie, from Google, calling to give you some tips for getting more traffic to your website." I get these calls, too, and at least can understand Julie. Worse are the calls from Hamid in Pakistan who "has a sure-fire way to get your website to the first page of Google next month."

If this were 2005, I could almost believe him. Back then the competition for high-value keywords and internet real estate was nearly non-existent. In many cases, you could publish a website and have it on the first page of a search engine in a few weeks. Not anymore!

Consider some basic facts:

- 90% of the content on the Internet has been created since 2016
- 3.5 billion Google searches are conducted every minute
- There are 1.3 billion websites on the internet, and growing every day

The process of getting found online, also called search engine optimization (SEO), has spawned a whole industry. Literally thousands of companies throughout the world offer this service exclusively. Add to that a library full of books on the subject, and it's no wonder that as a business owner it can seem overwhelming.

It is not my intent in this chapter to add to that confusion. The reality is that much of what I might write could be out of date in 90 days, as the search engines surprise us with an algorithm change. Rather, I want to arm you with enough basic information to understand how the search engines process information and display websites in the search results. This will also help you ask the right questions as you talk with possible vendors for this service.

To more quickly understand the world of getting found and displayed by the search engines, think of two trees. They are of equal height and girth, and each has an extensive root system. One tree is the work you will do when building and maintaining your website to maximize its exposure. This is called "onsite" optimization and should be an ongoing process that will keep the search engine spiders crawling and updating your site.

The other tree represents the "offsite" efforts designed to accomplish the same goal. I mentioned the root system because numerous techniques and strategies are available for you to employ for both onsite and offsite optimization. In the next few pages I'll go into some detail of what the roots under each of these trees look like.

But first, you should have some understanding of how the search engines work. Search engines – and there are many of them – all perform the same function. They scour billions of pieces of content and evaluate thousands of considerations in an effort to determine which will most closely meet the needs of the person typing in the search query.

Search engines (and I'll use "Google" as a general term to encompass all of them) accomplish this by discovering and cataloguing all of the content on the internet using a process known as "crawling and indexing." The slang expression for the "bots" that do this work is "spiders." Another term you might have heard and should be familiar with is "SERPs." This stands for Search Engine Results Pages that are displayed by Google in answer to the search terms entered by the searcher.

A "paid" search result is one that you see at the top of the page. There are frequently four of these, and they are designated by the work "AD" next to them. An "organic" search result is the websites that you see further down the page in the search results. Many searches will also have a "map pack" of three or four businesses that are featured just under the paid ads. Many times there is a dropdown menu that you can click on and see more local vendors in the category you are searching for.

How does the search engine prioritize the websites that are displayed in response to a search? That is a closely guarded secret, proprietary to each search engine. While the specifics of their algorithms might be classified, the search engines provide regular updates to agencies who are involved with optimizing webpages, giving us strong clues for the best practices they are looking for. Those reports and conversations with our Google representatives are the basis for what I'm sharing with you about getting found online.

On-Site Optimization

Whether you are building a new website or have one that is several years old, you can implement a number of actions to help the search engines present it more frequently. Here are several of the most effective:

Site Speed: Google knows how impatient people are and has developed a separate tool for website owners that enables them to know what the user experience is. The tool is called Page Speed Online and is available in any browser at any time. If you have a WordPress website, a simple fix to increase load speed is to delete unused plugins.

Essential Tags: You might have heard the expression "meta tags" and not been certain what it referred to. Meta tags are the snippets of content that describe your page's content. They don't appear on the page of your site itself, only in the page's source code. These are important because they are how Google understands information about your webpage. There are two essential tags:

- Title Tags define the title of your webpage. The spiders read the first 60 characters only.
- Meta Description (160 characters max) is how the search engines understand what you are writing about and the audience they should send your content to.

Content to Drive Traffic: Most websites are written like a tri-fold brochure. That is, the content focuses on features and benefits of the product/service being offered. Customer focus groups are telling us that this is no longer enough. Instead, they want to see content that:

- Is interesting to read
- Is in-depth and well written
- Is written with the user in mind
- Solves a problem
- Is easy to share
- Is optimized for a high-volume keyword

The challenge in creating content is striking a balance between including the keywords that will bring a prospect to your website with understanding and appealing to the searcher's intent—the reason why the user is searching that particular keyword.

Content Quality: You might remember two of the major updates to Google's algorithm, known as Panda and Hummingbird. The focus of both was to incentivize website owners to write and offer better-quality content. Two lessons from these updates are clear. First, avoid low-quality, generic content that doesn't speak directly to the needs of the user. Second, write longer articles. How long? At least 1,500 words!

Let me qualify this with some "real-world" practical experience. Most business websites are updated infrequently. You might put up new images of jobs occasionally or add information on one of your products/services, but you are not writing long-form articles for publication on your site. Once your website incorporates the best onsite practices, you should focus on offsite techniques unless you have a desire, and the time, to consistently write a blog.

Navigation: Does your site make it easy for the search engine spiders to find all your pages and content? The spiders find their way around the web by following links. If you have pages that do not link to other pages on your website, they are essentially invisible. Remember, the spiders do not crawl forms or read text within images. A way to make things easier for the spiders is to have an XML sitemap added to your site. This is a plug-in on WordPress as well as other site-building platforms.

NAP: If you run a local business it is important to include your Name, Address, and Phone several times on your website. The easiest way to do this is having them in the footer of the site. This will be at the bottom of every page. If your current website doesn't have a footer section, get back with your developer and insist they add one. This is also the place to put links to your Privacy Policy and Terms of Service, two other documents important to the search engines.

Header Tags, Internal Links, Anchor Text, etc.: Now we're getting pretty granular, beyond the scope of what I want to do in this chapter. These terms refer to HTML codes that are used on your website to help the search engine spiders navigate. They are important!

HTML, CSS, JavaScript: There's one last bit of tech-speak you should be aware of as you talk with your website developer or someone you're interviewing to help your search engine positioning. These three terms are related to how your site is created and made accessible. HTML stands for hypertext markup language and is the backbone of your website. Elements of your site like headings, paragraphs, lists, and content are all defined in the HTML code.

CSS defines how your website looks. It is an acronym for 'cascading style sheets' and is why your site has certain fonts, colors, and page appearance. HTML was created to describe content rather than style it. With the advent of CSS, webpages could be beautified without the cumbersome process of manually coding each page.

JavaScript helps a website 'behave" dynamically. That is, it helps a page become interactive. JavaScript can enable a popup to appear or reach out to a third-party resource and display an ad on your page. Occasionally JavaScript can create issues with aspects of your site not being visible to the spiders.

Schema Markup: With more and more pages being uploaded to the internet, in 2016 the primary search engines collaborated on a plan to more quickly classify the information that is on a webpage. The result of this effort was schema markup. There are literally thousands of schema markups, but here's the bottom line. Let's say you've written an 8,000-word article on how to plant a rosebush. How does the spider identify the author, steps in the process, fertilizers you mention, different types of roses, and more that is in your article? Answer: Schema. Schema is a way you can organize or label your content so the search engines have a better understanding of what elements on your web pages are.

If all of this sounds complicated, well, it is. If you are a growing business in a competitive market (which describes just about all of us!), then incorporating these on-site techniques is critical to your website getting found and displayed.

However, once these things have been finished, the only way to continue with online techniques is by regularly publishing content. To go beyond that you must focus on offsite work. For a newer website it is the off-site optimization that will help your site compete against the more seasoned sites that dominate the first two pages.

Off-Site Optimization

Off-page optimization of your website is simply defined as any effort undertaken outside of your website to improve its position in search results. More than this obvious difference is the fact that the on-page strategies I just shared are totally within your control. That is not always the case with your off-site efforts. The most recent article I can find from our Google rep indicates that their search algorithm contains more than 270 components. These reflect both on- and off-site work. While we can't know exactly which of their criteria is the most important, we can draw some general conclusions based on testing done by organizations like Moz and Ahrefs.

Reputation: What others say about your business as reflected in reviews is critical. I have a chapter devoted to this so won't go into detail here.

Referring Domains: You might be familiar with the term "backlinks." This refers to a link from another website back to your website. These are considered the most important asset you can build for your website and have been a key component of Google's algorithm for years. In general, a page with more backlinks will rank higher than one with fewer backlinks. The caveat is that you want your links to come from sites with a high page authority. Low-authority links are not as valuable.

Link Juice: When a webpage links to any of your articles or your website's home page it passes "link juice." This link juice helps with the ranking of an article as well as improving the domain authority. Related to this are the terms "do-follow" and "no-follow." The link provider can indicate to the search engine spiders that this like can be "followed," taking the spider to your website. A no-follow link does not pass link juice and has limited value.

Linking Root Domain: Google monitors how many incoming links originate from a unique domain. No matter how many times it might link to your site, it will count as only one link for ranking purposes.

Low-Quality Links: There is an open marketplace for the purchase of links. However, this is not the easy answer you might think. The search engines look carefully at the sources of your links. If they come from harvested sites or spam or porn sites they will actually count against your site. (This change was enacted with the Penguin update in 2012).

Broken Link: This is a link to a website that no longer exists. It is normally a negative to have this link; however, there is a more sophisticated optimization strategy that involves identifying these sites, buying them, and recreating links from them. That is beyond the scope of this chapter, but we have used this on behalf of clients with great success.

Google Business Page: While not a direct off-site optimization strategy, your GMB page is the cornerstone of your business presence online. Particularly since early-2019, Google has been placing increased emphasis on the accuracy of this page. More important is the ability to upload posts with images and links. You could load a new post every day if you want (we have done this for a brand-new website and found that it climbed in the search results far faster than we expected). Google "expires" posts after 7 days but rewards the website of companies that consistently post quality content.

Citations and Directory Sites: There are more than 3,000 of these, many of which you are probably familiar with. Sites like Yelp, Manta, and YellowPages are examples of citation and directory sites. "Claiming" your listing on these sites and making sure the information is accurate is important, since the spiders crawl these sites and link back to your website from them. These citations are also called "NAP" because they include your business name, address, and phone number.

How many to claim? This is another case where quality trumps quantity. You want to claim the dozen or so major directories, any that might be specific to your industry, as well as those in your local market. I also like to analyze a client's competitors and see what directory sites they are registered on and make sure we claim those as well. In general, somewhere in the 50 to 80 sites range should be enough.

Press Release: This is a strategy for generating high-quality backlinks and might be different than you think. This is not writing an article for the local paper and asking them to print it (although that too has value.) A press release in this context is written to highlight something about you, your company, a product or service, a convention or speaking engagement – really, almost any reason. The release is then submitted to a press organization for consideration and distribution. Since the distribution goes to print, television, and web-based news agencies, the links that can be created are excellent. We use a service with more than 5,000 outlets and find that quarterly press releases have helped our clients rank more quickly and sustain their place in the search results.

Click-Through Rate: This is simple arithmetic. How many times is your website presented in the search results and clicked on by the searcher? That's your click-through rate. If your site is on page six of the results, of course there is almost no chance it will be found. There are strategies to augment this result that are within Google's terms of service, so it is still possible to overcome a lower page rank.

Dwell Time: This is an important metric in Google's eyes. When someone comes to your website, how long do they stay there? Longer is better, because that indicates to Google that the searcher has found content that is valuable. (Do you know how long the average person stays on a website after entering a search term? Between 10 and 12 seconds! That's why dwell time is so important.)

Brand Mentions: Google calls these *express links* and refers to them in one of its patents. They recognize that frequently people mention a brand without creating a specific link to that brand's website. These references without a specific link are called *implied links*; if a link is created it is an *express link*.

Social Signals: These are mentions of your company on social media. Google says they do not consider these, although quite a lot of anecdotal evidence is offered trying to prove that they do. In this case I believe Google, for the simple reason that it is too easy to manipulate social media. I can go to any number of service providers (visit fiverr.com and you'll see dozens of them) and for a few dollars buy "likes" or social media mentions. Given Google's consistent emphasis on quality over quantity, I do not believe that social signals are valuable.

After reading through this you might be thinking that offline optimization of your website is even more difficult than the online work. That's probably true, if for no other reason than the fact that you can't directly control it. That is want makes it valuable: it's hard and it takes a consistent effort over time to see results.

I would be remiss if I didn't mention that traditional offline marketing measures can have an indirect impact on many of the factors I've mentioned. Consider the company that sends 10,000 postcards through the post office's Every Door Direct Mail program. It is likely that a significant number of the recipients of this card will have some interest in the company and its products and will go to their website. That increase in traffic from direct search, another Google metric, will enhance the site in Google's algorithm. If those visitors stay on the site for a minute or more, that impacts the Dwell Time metric. If they click on an information form and give their email address, or a click to call button and reach out to the company, even more "juice" flows. You get the idea.

Let me say again that this chapter is in no way an exhaustive study of all that is necessary to manage getting found online. Honestly, I've barely scratched the surface. But you should now be well armed to have a conversation with someone who does website optimization, ask good questions, and understand the answers.

"Why is it, a man wakes up in the morning after sleeping in an advertised bed, washes with an advertised soap, shaves with an advertised razor, sits down and drinks advertised coffee, and drives to work in an advertised car...then he refuses to advertise saying, "advertising doesn't pay?" But when his business fails, he finally advertises: 'Business for Sale.'"

--Anonymous

What Now?

If I've done my job well, you have made a lot of notes and have some exciting ideas for growing your business. What now? How can you translate that enthusiasm into taking steps to attract new customers, clients, or patients?

One of the first topics I discuss when sitting with a business owner for the first time is the capacity of their business. By that I mean how much can they reasonably invest in marketing at this time, and how many new prospects can their team handle next month?

For most of us as small business owners we don't have an extra five or seven thousand dollars sitting around to put into a marketing plan. Even if you did, I would likely advise against doing that all at once without being sure your team was ready to accept an influx of inquiries and new business. If you hired my firm to help you, and we brought you fifty new prospects next month, but you could only effectively work with twenty I have not done you a favor. There are thirty prospects out there who did not have a good experience, exactly what you don't want!

The first step then in implementing a new marketing strategy is to see what you can reasonably afford to start with. Since none of us have the budget of Amazon we must prioritize. Over time, as new business is generated, we can add additional marketing tools and continue the growth. If you're talking with an agency who is not willing to accept you on this basis then keep looking!

What should your priorities be? We advise business owners to consider implementing in this order:

1. Do you have a basic website that is getting visitors each month? If so, then leave this as is for the time being and work on other priorities. If you do not have a website then you must start here. A business is not considered "credible" in the mind of the prospect if they can't find your website.

2. The next priority is your reputation online. Just as your website tells a prospect you have a credible company, your reputation provides the social proof from previous customers that yours is a good company to work with.

3. Third, traffic. You have a website and a good reputation, now it's time to announce it to more people. The best way to do this is through paid traffic. As I share in the chapter on this topic banner ads for both retargeting and cold traffic campaigns are the best value in today's market.

4. The next option depends on your ideal customer profile. If many of your customers are searching on social media for vendors and company information, then putting a social media program in place is where you should focus next.

    If that is not the case then prioritize building out your sales funnel(s) with multiple offers, landing pages, and campaigns targeted at specific niches of customers.

5. Finally, implement more sophisticated strategies designed to help you get found online more easily. I know this seems counterintuitive to the constant phone calls and emails you are probably getting with offers to put your website on page one of Google. I'm certainly not minimizing the value of that positioning. Realistically it takes time, frequently nine to twelve months, to see significant progress in movement for your most important keywords. It can also be expensive as you'll need to be pursuing multiple strategies at the same time.

You might notice that the order of priorities I've just suggested mirrors the chapter organization in this book. That is not an accident.

One of the reasons I wrote this book is to encourage you to consider engaging our company, The Alchemy Consulting Group, as your partner in growing your business. Since 2003 that has been our focus. At that time, if you remember, the Internet was not the dominant force it is today. YouTube had not been invented. Most of us were still using dial up if we were online at all, and who knew what a "Google" was?

A lot has changed in how we help our clients grow their businesses. What hasn't changed is the core value that has been our mantra from the beginning, *"We Want to be Your 'In House' Marketing Department."* On the next page I'll share answers to some of the frequently asked questions we receive from our prospects. Maybe you have some of the same questions and will find this helpful.

Whether you talk with our company or someone else, I encourage you to strongly consider getting some outside expertise as you design your marketing plans. As a business owner you are deeply immersed in the day to day of running the company. A fresh pair of eyes, trained in the most current business growth strategies, can be invaluable and pay for itself many times over.

A couple of times in the earlier chapters I've mentioned a free consulting hour. I was serious about this. If you'd like to take me up on this offer please send an email to gordon@thealchemyconsultinggroup.com with the subject line: Free Consult. I'll reply with a short survey and ask you to complete and return so I can know more about your company and be prepared to offer you the most value during this hour. I really enjoy these conversations, and don't try to "sell" you, so I hope you'll take me up on this offer.

One final invitation. Please take a minute and visit www.AlchemyCore5.com. This is a part of our funnel and will give you access to additional information about each of the services we offer as well as some of our 'trust triggers."

The 11 Most Asked Questions About Working with The Alchemy Consulting Group

1. So Who is The Alchemy Consulting Group?

Alchemy is a strategic marketing and business growth consulting firm started in 2003 by Gordon Van Wechel. Prior to launching Alchemy, Gordon built and sold three national companies in three different industries. Many of our associate consultants are also experienced business owners. That means we know what it's like to work 80 hours a week and "wear all the hats" in the business.

Unlike most ad agencies or more traditional consulting firms, Alchemy has created a menu of services, we call them the "Core 5®." These have been designed to provide our clients with specific solutions to their business growth challenges regardless of how long you might have been in business. Whether you are the owner of a new business just starting out, or have an established company looking to expand, we can offer tools and strategies to help you take the next step. The benefit to you is that we don't expect you to fit into our "marketing mold." We will be able to help you evaluate exactly what you need, and can afford, at this time in your business.

2. Why Do I Even Need a Consultant?

Every great sports star, businessperson, and entertainment superstar is surrounded by coaches and advisors. As the world of business moves faster and gets more competitive, it can be difficult to keep up with the changes in your industry as well as the innovations in marketing and management.

Having a business growth consultant is no longer a luxury; it's become a necessity.

If you're honest, you know that it is almost impossible to get an objective answer from yourself. That is not to say that you cannot survive in business without a consultant, but it's almost impossible to thrive.

A consultant can see the forest for the trees. A consultant will make you focus on the game, making you run more laps than you feel like. A consultant will tell it like it really is. A consultant will give you small pointers. A consultant will listen to and understand your pain. A consultant will help you remember the dreams you had when going into business...and help you get back on track to achieving them.

3. OK, so What is the First Step?

We'll ask you to complete our Marketing Audit. This is a series of questions, most of them are simple Yes/No answers, but there are several questions that will require a more detailed response. The purpose of the audit is to help you pinpoint areas of strength in your marketing now and help identify those aspects of your plan that could use further work. A common experience of people participating in this exercise is a lot of ideas and excitement about what can be done to bring in more customers and profits. It will also prompt some questions about specific marketing tactics and how to implement them.

Once you have returned your audit, we'll schedule a time to meet. This typically is a 60 to 90-minute conversation where we help you dig deeper into the level your company is performing at today, and where you'd like it to be in twelve months. It is also an opportunity for you to get to know us a little more and see if working together makes sense. At the end of this meeting, at your request, we will prepare a proposal detailing our recommendations specific to your company, and the investment you will be making. You can then decide when you'd like to begin.

There is no charge for this initial meeting.

4. What Will You Do, and How Long Will It Take?

Just as every person is different, we believe each business is different. The plan that we suggest for your business will be based on the evaluation we make after reviewing your Marketing Audit and the conversation we have in the initial meeting. Which is to say that I cannot give you a specific idea of what we will do in your business, because we haven't designed your plan yet.

I can tell you that while about 80% of our strategic marketing focus today is online, we still incorporate traditional offline tools like direct mail, radio, and television marketing. We do that because they work. The particular mix of strategies for your company will depend on your goals, current situation, budget, competitive landscape, and personnel available to handle an influx of new customers.

As far as how long a typical program might take, we like to make commitments in 12- month increments. We don't try to lock someone in a contract saying that, but the plan we design for you will be based on a year of implementation.

If you've been in business for more than a few months you've already seen, and maybe even purchased, one or more so called "quick fixes." Most consultants want you to believe that they can solve your business growth problems in a few days. Our philosophy at Alchemy is that establishing a foundation for long term success in your business means not just scraping the surface with a few "Google secrets." We prefer to design a multi-channel marketing strategy that offers you controlled growth. That means implementing one or two modules initially, then, as they pay for themselves, adding more marketing. Over the course of a year, working together, we help you fully capitalize on current markets for your product/service, and extend the reach of your company into new areas.

5. How Do You Know This Will Work in My Industry?

Really simple. Our team of consultants are experts in sales, marketing, business development, management strategies, hiring key people, and evaluation of markets; just to name a few of their competencies. With more than 250 business building tactics in our arsenal you will quickly see how effective and powerful our modules are.

Add to this the fact that we have consulted with more than 300 companies in over 50 business categories and you can see that very likely that we have worked in a business that is the same or very similar to yours.

6. How Much Time and Money will This Cost Me?

The first couple of months your involvement in the processes will require more time. That might be review of copy or collateral materials, training your team in a new sales system, or regularly scheduled update meetings you'll have with one of our team members. The actual implementation of tactics, what we call the "back office fulfillment" duties, are all done by one of our groups of specialists. If part of your program calls for a revision of your website, the actual work will be done by our web builders. If you are doing a paid advertising program, then another of our teams will handle the day to day details of that marketing channel for you.

As to the financial investment...well, nothing! That is if you look at it from the same perspective as we do. That's the difference between a cost and an investment. Everything we propose for your company is a true investment in your future. Not only will you create great results in your business, but you'll learn more than just marketing strategies. Working with our consultants will give you an education from experienced entrepreneurs you could never get in school, and this is knowledge that you can repeat over and over.

Just so you don't think I'm dodging the question, let me give you a range. We have clients who invest as little as $500 monthly and others who spend $10,000 a month. It will depend on your company, budget, short- and long-term growth goals, and how aggressively you want to pursue them.

7. Are There Any Guarantees?

Will all of your business goals be met by working with us? Maybe, or maybe not. We will never promise any specific result, nor can we guarantee that any of your goals will become a reality. The bottom line is we are your consultants, but it is still your business and it's up to you and your team to take the sales opportunities we bring you and convert those prospects to customers and eventually to raving fans of your business.

Only *you* can be fully accountable for your success. We guarantee to give you the best service we can, the benefit of all our experience and proven business growth strategies, and to encourage and even cajole you to reach for your goals. But at the end of the day it is your business.

Here is the guarantee that we do offer. When we work with you to design a strategic plan we'll define some clear goals that should be achieved within the first four months of working together. If they have not been achieved in that time period then we will continue to work with you at no charge until those goals have been met.

8. You're Based in Another City, How Does That Work?

You may have read Thomas Friedman's book from a few years ago called "The World Is Flat." His point was that with the communication tools available today business has truly become international. Even the shoe store down the street can have an ecommerce website or a store on eBay and sell to the whole world. Our business is living proof of that new reality: 80% of our clients live in another state. We regularly supply them with reports and updates via email, and schedule progress review conversations using phone or Zoom online conference.

Occasionally a client will want us to be at their location for a specific purpose, but generally that is an expense that you don't need to incur.

9. Do You Just Help with My Marketing?

While our primary focus is on marketing and business growth strategies, we'll help you in other areas too. For example, part of our Reputation Marketing module includes a training program helping your staff become more adept at customer service. I mentioned earlier the concept of the "inside reality" of your company, we'll help you identify operations within your business that can be improved.

We strongly believe in systems, the more you can implement systems in your business the better you can run your business instead of having it run you!

10. When is The Best Time to Get Started?

Yesterday. Really.

OK, right now, today; before you take another marketing step, waste another dollar, lose another sale, work another 80-hour week.

Far too many businesspeople wait and see. They confuse activity with accomplishment and think that working harder will make it all better. Remember, what you know got you to where you are. To get to where you want to go you've got to make some changes and most likely learn something new.

There is no time like the present to get started on your dreams and goals.

11. How Do I Start?

Call us toll free at 877-978-2110 and ask for a Marketing Audit. You'll be connected with one of our consultants who will help you get started. We'll set up a time for an interview so we can learn about your business. Then we'll work with you to create a plan that helps you achieve your goals on a timeline that is affordable and makes sense for your business.

This may seem like a big job at the beginning, but with an Alchemy Consultant you'll have someone guiding you each step of the way.

About the Author

Gordon Van Wechel is an entrepreneur who has built three national companies, each in a different industry. He has written seven previous books, two of which became Amazon top sellers, and has been cited by all four of the major television networks as an expert in business marketing.

Gordon is a frequent speaker to business groups, and he teaches a marketing class to new business owners on behalf of the Service Corps of Retired Executives division of the Small Business Administration.

In addition to his own enterprises, he has travelled extensively in Asia, Africa, and the Middle East on behalf of several non-governmental organizations. His work there has focused on micro-enterprise programs that, to date, have resulted in the creation of over five hundred successful businesses, seventeen village schools, and numerous community development projects.

He is the founder and President of The Alchemy Consulting Group, a marketing strategy and business-growth firm started in 2003 and based in Chesapeake, VA. Other offices are in Austin, TX and Albuquerque, NM.

Other Books by Gordon Van Wechel

The Capture Your Neighborhood Formula,

Ten Vital Questions
    First Edition: 2010; Second Edition: 2015

Total Market Takeover® For Your Roofing Business
    First Edition: 2014; Second Edition: 2018

Total Market Takeover® For Your Professional Practice
    Co-Author Jennine Michael

www.ingramcontent.com/pod-product-compliance
Lightning Source LLC
Chambersburg PA
CBHW070412220526
45465CB00010B/295